What consulting firm leaders have to say about working with David A. Fields...

David's coaching and training is extremely applicable and real, something our staff loves, and that is huge for implementation. No academic or theoretical approaches, just real business. For me personally, as CEO, David is very proactive, helps me always think forward and keeps pushing the firm upwards! Working with David is a huge win!

—Jonas Pedersén, PhD, CEO, Deallus Consulting

We considered many different business development advisors, including some of the best-known providers in the world, and David distinguished himself within the first couple minutes of our introduction call. His approach is simple, focused, and powerful. It's clear that by using David's methods we are on course to being a stronger organization, being better consultants and, most importantly, providing better service to our clients.

—Sami Ibrahim, Principal and CEO, Agility Solutions

All I can say about David is that everything he said would work that we tried has worked. We followed David's process when talking to a large prospect a few weeks back and the results were amazing. NEVER in my professional life has a presentation of mine been so well accepted. Not a single dissenting voice! Not one. I can't thank David enough for transforming our practice.

—Chris Doig, CEO, Wayferry, Inc.

David's consulting sales prowess is amazing. He showed us the finer points of how to market our business and make a successful sales call. We landed a huge new account within weeks of starting with David.

—Bob Endres, CEO, Synaptic Decisions

Mission accomplished! David is exceptionally resourceful, proactive, and thinks creatively. I thoroughly enjoyed personally working with David. He is highly, highly responsive and did a great job for us.

—Gadi Saarony, Worldwide Head, Parexel Consulting

Plain and simple, David's strategies work. I am taking these results to the bank. Utilizing his expertise and guidance, I quickly covered my investment with him many times over.

—Tom Borg, CEO, Tom Borg Consulting

David helped my company bring in projects at higher fees and set our sights on making a much more significant impact—and being compensated for that. Thanks to David, the gross revenue on our latest project is about seven times larger than the typical engagement we used to handle. Perhaps more importantly, his impact continues year after year. Last year our gross revenue grew by over 50% and we're set on tripling this year by using techniques straight out of David's playbook.

—Jaime Campbell, Co-Founder and CFO, Tier One Services

David helped us focus beyond providing great value to clients to building a sustainable practice that will provide great value long into the future.

—Scott Thompson, Co-founder, Acceleration Point

I invited David to talk at our Unanet Champions Conference, and even consultants who struggle with government contracts gave him rave reviews.

—Fran Craig, CEO, Unanet

Our program with David was worth every penny. We truly enjoyed it and found much more benefit to our practice than we originally anticipated.

—John Foster, CEO, Bedford & Main

Our ability to close business for higher fees has improved more from each hour spent with David than from years of reading marketing books and sitting through sales training classes. Today we negotiated a contract the way he showed us last week and doubled our normal rates!

—Jamie Broughton, CEO, Footprint Leadership

David helped me transition from a corporate executive to owning a 6-figure consulting practice with room to grow. His training and perspectives provided many shortcuts, but perhaps even more critically, helped me avoid multiple miss-steps that may have blindsided my transition. I am both relieved for his help and grateful.

—Wm. David Levesque, President,
Lean Performance Development, Inc

David offers the kind of advice that makes you want to run out of your seat and apply it immediately because it makes such brilliant sense. As an added bonus, he shares generously and with humor. I'm always eager to hear more.

—Young Mi Park, Chair, Executive Circle,
NY American Marketing Association

David, we just landed our first huge client and we have you to thank for this! We've already had our new consultants start going through your materials so they can learn what I've been learning from you.

— Adam Cooper, Partner, Ascent Consulting

David quickly hones in on exactly what we need and articulates it in a memorable, actionable way. While other coaches have vague ideas, David's ideas are pithy and practical. As a result of our work together, I have greater confidence going after larger projects and my firm is in more conversations for larger projects than ever before.

— Kaihan Krippendorff, CEO, Outthinker

The Irresistible Consultant's

GUIDE to WINNING CLIENTS

The Irresistible Consultant's

GUIDE to
WINNING
CLIENTS

6 Steps to Unlimited Clients &
Financial Freedom

DAVID A. FIELDS

NEW YORK

NASHVILLE • MELBOURNE • VANCOUVER

The Irresistible Consultant's Guide to Winning Clients
6 Steps to Unlimited Clients & Financial Freedom

Published in New York, New York, by Morgan James Publishing. Morgan James and The Entrepreneurial Publisher are trademarks of Morgan James, LLC. www.MorganJamesPublishing.com

The Morgan James Speakers Group can bring authors to your live event. For more information or to book an event visit The Morgan James Speakers Group at www.TheMorganJamesSpeakersGroup.com.

ISBN 978-1-68350-164-0 paperback
ISBN 978-1-68350-165-7 eBook
Library of Congress Control Number: 2016911848

In an effort to support local communities, raise awareness and funds, Morgan James Publishing donates a percentage of all book sales for the life of each book to Habitat for Humanity Peninsula and Greater Williamsburg.

Get involved today! Visit
www.MorganJamesBuilds.com

For my beautiful sons, Mitchel and Jeremy.

Acknowledgments & Attributions

Isaac Newton said, "If I have seen further, it is by standing on the shoulders of giants." That is most certainly an apt metaphor for me. My journey in consulting and understanding of how to win business springboards off an unbelievable platform of knowledge and ideas developed by others. A few people in particular deserve special mention:

Bob Endres is a pioneer in using risk management principles outside of conventional settings. While I had heard of presenting alternatives in contracts before, Bob's work truly showed me the opportunity for offering trades, reallocating risk and viewing proposals as an extension of the discovery process.

Jeff Hill was a co-founder of the boutique firm where I started my consulting career in 1997. You'll see Jeff's influence scattered throughout the book. A couple of notable instances are the practice of "walking the halls" to generate business and "making dust fly" once a project is signed.

Marshall Goldsmith is an inspiration to millions of people around the world. His careful, diligent, relentless attention to building his firm has served as a map during many parts of my journey.

Keith Ferrazzi is the author of several, outstanding bestsellers, including *Never Eat Alone*. Keith is not only a fascinating person to know; he's a master of meeting people and cultivating relationships. Among the numerous, Keith-inspired messages in this book are my recommendations on making the most of conferences.

Alan Weiss is unquestionably one of the most brilliant and eloquent people in the consulting arena, and certainly the most prolific. Many ideas I learned elsewhere were articulated more clearly by Weiss, including value-based fees. You'll hear echoes of Weiss's approaches, turns of phrase, and ideas in many chapters. Perhaps most notable is the proposal structure. Also, the Context Discussion, which extends (in important ways) off of Weiss's practice of gaining agreement from prospects to Objectives, Metrics and Value.

Randall Munroe is the author of xkcd.com, a hysterically funny look at life, love and geeky stuff. I've never talked with Randall and have no idea of his thoughts on consulting; however, if you visit his site you'll immediately see where I first learned to draw stick figures! For the record, I drew 99% of the illustrations in this book myself, from scratch on a blank computer screen.

Plus, of course, there are the many, many consultants I've had the honor to coach and who, in turn, have taught me countless lessons. I am humbled by the thousands of consultants in my "community" who share their wisdom with me and each other.

The content of this book was enhanced by dozens of beta readers. The structure was improved immeasurably by Jonathan Verney, and the readability was enhanced by my editor, Linda Cashdan. You're holding a book in your hands thanks largely to the efforts of my marketing team, spearheaded by Raoul Davis and Tina LoSasso.

Finally, I owe an unfathomable debt to my colleague, editor, friend, lover, and life partner, Robin. Without her input, twelve chapters would have been incomprehensible and another dozen chapters of critical material would have been omitted. So, come to think of it, you may owe her a Thank You too!

Contents

STEP 1: Think Right-Side Up
(Prepare Yourself to Succeed)

STEP 2: Maximize Impact
(Find Your Killer Offering)

STEP 3: Build Visibility
(Become Known by Your Prospects)

STEP 4: Connect, Connect, Connect
(Create Relationships and Opportunities)

STEP 5: Become the Obvious Choice
(Emerge as an Irresistible Solution)

STEP 6: Propose, Negotiate & Close
(Enjoy the Payoff)

I've learned why clients bring in consultants, and why they choose the ones they choose. I've witnessed their deepest frustrations, as well as their fears and hopes and dreams. My first book, *The Executive's Guide to Consultants* (McGraw-Hill, 2012), has helped clients around the world do a better job of selecting consultants. This book will help you do a better job of getting selected!

I know what *both* sides are looking for and why there's such a huge gap. Most importantly, though, I know how to close that gap so an exquisite project falls right into the consultant's lap. Your lap.

The Six Steps

Here's a quick summary of the simple, practical steps you'll practice on your way to unlimited clients and financial freedom:

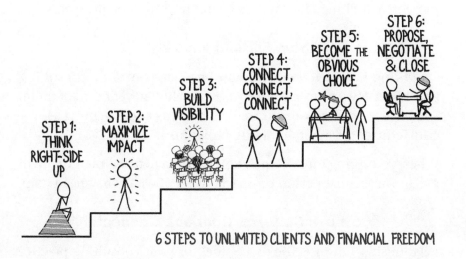

6 STEPS TO UNLIMITED CLIENTS AND FINANCIAL FREEDOM

Step 1: Think "Right-Side Up"

First, you're going to revamp how you perceive yourself as a consultant by, ironically, thinking less about yourself! You'll shift from thinking about *your* services and *your* expertise and *your* problem-solving skills to thinking about your *prospects'* problems, needs, and situation.

You'll begin to see yourself and your prospects with a new set of eyes that will effectively quiet the negative self-talk that plagues many consulting professionals. Plus, you'll learn how a simple but critical change in your internal dialogue will help you gain massive confidence.

Step 2: Maximize Impact

Of course, before you start confidently shouting out to prospects, you have to make sure they'll listen! There's little point in ratcheting up your marketing if no one is paying attention to what you say.

That's why, in Step 2, you'll clarify your target and offering in a way you've probably never considered before. You'll identify the Right People, the Right Problem, and the Right Solution, then encapsulate those in a "Fishing Line" that is guaranteed to hook prospects.

Step 3: Build Visibility

One thing I can tell you with absolute certainty is no consulting firm has ever won business from a client who's never heard of them. You have to become known. Step 3 is creating and executing a powerful, efficient visibility-building program.

When you spring off of Step 3, you'll own a detailed plan that will make you the first person prospects think of when they need help.

Step 4: Connect, Connect, Connect

Relationship power is the rocket fuel for your consulting practice (and life). No one buys a $100,000 consulting project with an "add to cart" button, which is why creating strong connections with decision makers is critical.

In Step 4, you'll create relationships, nurture them, and use "The Turn" to leverage those relationships into rich opportunities.

Step 5: Become the Obvious Choice

As your relationships evolve into active leads, you'll engage in dialogues designed to uncover exactly what will prompt your prospect to sign on the dotted line. In consulting, you are never the only choice. But in Step 5 you'll use the "Context Discussion"—the one conversation that renders competition moot, and exponentially multiplies your ability to close a project.

Step 6: Propose, Negotiate & Close

The final step is one easy, smooth action where you enjoy the payoff from your previous efforts. You'll write perfect proposals, effortlessly handle objections, deal with minor and major pricing issues, and negotiate like a seven-figure pro.

Most importantly, you'll consistently win more projects from more clients and earn some serious dough!

Making it Work for You

Speaking of dough, it's going to be a running theme throughout this book. To make the ideas in this book more concrete, I created a fictional prospect named Mr. Yuri Yusimi (pronounced *you-see-me*). Yusimi is a plant manager at (what else?) a bakery firm called Sereus Dough Inc.

xviii | **THE IRRESISTIBLE CONSULTANT'S GUIDE TO WINNING CLIENTS**

It just so happens that Yusimi has a problem that he will pay the right consultant oodles of money to solve—and I want that consultant to be *YOU*.

Every tip, tool, technique, and script I'm going to give you to win a project from Yusimi and Sereus Dough will work for you, no matter the focus of your consulting practice, and no matter your target's industry, function, or position.

And every step we take together is going to make you a better, wealthier, more irresistible consultant.

Bonus Materials

There are so many tips, techniques, templates, exercises, and examples I want to give you that this could easily have expanded into an unwieldy, monster wedding cake of a book—yummy, but tough to bring on a plane. The solution was to slim it down to a fat-free Danish and include plenty of delicious extras as bonus materials that are available online at davidafields.com/winningclients. All the bonus materials are free and easy to access.

Now, are you hungry for more clients? Good. Let's begin...

Think Right-Side Up

(Prepare Yourself to Succeed)

When we thought the sun revolved around the earth,
our vision was limited to a tiny planet. Then, a startling reversal
of perspective opened up a universe of possibilities.

Your journey to unlimited clients and financial freedom starts
with a similar, fundamental change in your frame of reference.
And it turns out your opportunities are boundless.

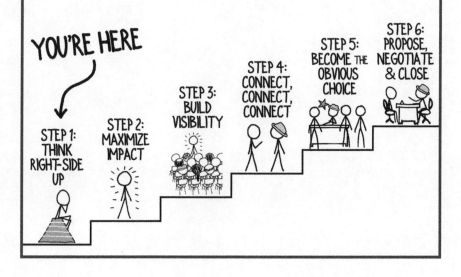

CHAPTER 1

Right-Side Up Thinking

This book is all about YOU and your practice. About YOU winning a steady stream of new clients, month in and month out. About *You* learning six steps that will take you from wherever you are today to being a happier, more confident, wealthier consultant. That's incredibly ironic, given your first lesson on the path to Nirvana:

Consulting isn't about YOU. It's about THEM.

If you put this book down now, after only learning—and fully adopting—that one concept, you'll walk away a far more successful consultant. (But please, keep reading!)

As normal, healthy human beings,* our world view looks like an upside down pyramid. In fact, it looks like the one on the next page.

---

* A healthy human being is anyone who likes dessert.

3

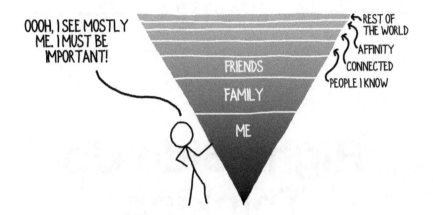

Most of our world view is dominated by a tiny group of one: it's only us. That's where we focus the majority of our thoughts. Then we spread our attention to the slightly larger groups comprising our family and friends. If we broaden our outlook further, we attend to acquaintances and other connections. Even though those are much broader populations, they tend to be obscured by the people closest to us. The rest of the world is way off there in the murky distance.

It's natural to think about yourself first. In fact, I'm glad you do, because thinking about yourself is what motivated you to pick up this book!

But from the perspective of attracting clients, that pyramid is upside down. To kick your business development into overdrive, *invert* your pyramid, and adopt Right-Side Up thinking. Put *them* first.

The Power of Right-Side Up Thinking

Let's look at a conversation between a fictional consultant named Bob and the equally fictional prospect you're going to be winning a project from throughout this book—Yuri Yusimi.

—vvvvv—

BOB: "Hi, uh, Mr. Yusimi. I'm Bob Jenkins from TopNotch Consulting."

YURI YUSIMI: "Good to meet you, Bob. What is it you guys do?"

BOB: "We help companies grow. I see you're with Sereus Dough, Inc. We've helped many companies just like Sereus improve their operations and profitability. We have access to some of the world's leading experts in all areas of manufacturing, and we've developed a breakthrough process called 9-T testing to identify exactly how to increase margins. I think Sereus Dough would be a great client. Here's my card. Can I give you a call to follow up?"

YURI YUSIMI: "Uh, thanks. Well, I have your card. Let me reach out if I think there's something we can do together."

—vvvvv—

Pretty bad, right? You know there's virtually no chance Yusimi will call Bob. Ever. You could probably count a dozen different mistakes Bob made. But the one underlying, fundamental challenge Bob has is his mindset. He's thinking about himself. As a result, he's talking all about himself. B-o-r-i-n-g. Also, irrelevant. That's upside down thinking at work.

Right-Side Up thinking flips your focus from YOU to THEM.

Amazingly, this simple switch will be your key to winning new business, growing your consulting practice, boosting your confidence, and, ultimately, securing your financial freedom. If you're willing to *act* on Right-Side Up thinking, you'll become an irresistible resource to your clients and your prospects.

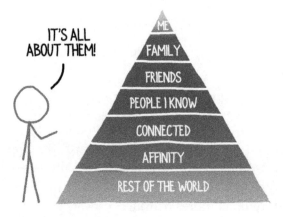

Since successful business development revolves around this core idea, you'll see it come up over and over again throughout this book. It affects everything you do as a consultant. Perhaps most importantly, Right-Side Up thinking will change how (and when) you think about yourself. And you're going to love the results.

The following table summarizes the difference between Right-Side Up thinking and typical "consultant-think".

Table 1-1

YOU ARE WHAT YOU THINK		
	Typical Consultant-Think	**Right-Side Up Thinking**
Mindset	Worry about what prospects think about you	Worry about what prospects think about themselves
Outreach Approach	Approaches you're comfortable with	Approaches they pay attention to
Marketing Materials	Your capabilities, your approaches, your offerings, your background	Their situation, their problems, their aspirations, their potential wins
Conversations	Your offering, getting business for you	Their world, helping them improve their lives
Offering	Your capabilities, your skill sets, your experience	Their needs, their wants

Every aspect of Right-Side Up thinking in Table 1-1 will be explored and expanded upon in the following chapters, so you'll have everything you need to make it work for you.

Right-Side Up thinking isn't rocket science. It's just common sense. But it's also the linchpin of your business development. If you embrace it, you'll be ahead of the game for the rest of your consulting life. If you reject it, you'll struggle.

How to Adopt Right-Side Up Thinking Instantly

Take a look at the opening line of your emails to prospects. Do they start with "I" language or with "You" language? Emails that start with "I" are less likely to engage a prospect, no matter how valuable or thoughtful the content may be.

A typical follow-up email might begin this way: "Hi Mr. Yusimi. I enjoyed meeting you yesterday."

Who's that email talking about? You! Does Yusimi care whether you enjoyed meeting him? Not really.

A simple shift makes the email feel a bit clunkier to you, but infinitely more interesting to Yusimi: "Hi Mr. Yusimi. You were a pleasure to meet yesterday..."

Now, who's the email about? Yusimi! It's a subtle difference, but it provides a big clue about your thinking. (And yes, I know your high school English teacher would pour red ink all over that opening line. Well, we ain't in English class.)

Move on to the body of your emails. What do you see? Are you talking about you or about him? Are you talking about what you want and what you have to offer, or are you talking about Mr. Yusimi's needs, his goals, and his situation?

Let's shift gears and examine your overall marketing communications. Does your marketing display typical consultant-think or is it overflowing with Right-Side Up thinking? How much "I" language fills your speeches and articles? Your answers will clue you in on your mindset. Chances are, you need to flip your thinking Right-Side Up.

"Hold on there, buckaroo," you may be muttering (if you believe consultants from Connecticut are cowboys, that is). "Don't stories about me make things more personal for prospects and allow me to create a deeper, more personal connection?" Good point. Personal stories *are* important. But it's a matter of balance and intention.

Think of it like a cocktail conversation. Your host starts talking about his recent trip to Italy, and Bob from TopNotch listens politely until the first pause, and then interjects, "That's great. That sounds just like my trip to Greece. I spoke to the Athenian Association of Feta Makers and… blah blah blah… it's all about me." (Well, Bob doesn't say that exactly, but that's what it sounds like.)

In contrast, because you're a master of Right-Side Up thinking, you listen attentively to your host (or Bob) for a good while before contributing anything. "That sounds great," you say. "Your adventure reminds me of my trip to France. The managerial style there was surprising. What did you think of the senior executives you met in Italy?" Just like that, you've shared something personal, connected to the other person, and kept the focus exactly where he wants it: on him.

Your business conversations and marketing work exactly the same way. Even during a speech, which tends to be a monologue rather than a dialogue, your stories can briefly reveal an endearing slice of yourself, then quickly revert to what it means for your audience. Why? Because even though your story is about you, the message is about them. It's always about *them*. That's Right-Side Up thinking.

From Hating Outreach to Loving It: Craig's Story

To see the power of Right-Side Up thinking in the real world, let's look at what transpired with a West Coast consultant named Craig. Craig quickly built a $300,000/year practice, despite the fact that he absolutely dreaded picking up the phone to make calls to prospects. Unfortunately, the well dried up after about five years (which is pretty common).

During every coaching session with Craig, he offered me a range of excuses for why he hadn't met his goals. He was perpetually shy of his objectives for outreach, for revenue... for pretty much everything. Craig hated picking up the phone. His confidence was shot, and he didn't know why anyone would listen to him. At this point, I asked Craig to walk me through some typical phone calls, and the problem stood out like a pro basketball player in a third-grade class:

Craig's prospect calls were all about *Craig*.

Craig wanted to make sure his prospects understood what he did and, if at all possible, he wanted to find out whether there was a project he could work on. It was locked in on him, him, him. It was Craig focused on Craig.

We turned Craig's phone calls Right-Side Up and shifted the focus to his prospects. He no longer worried one jot about what *he* had to say or whether *he* could surface a project. The goal was to connect, to attend to them and their needs and whatever was on their minds. Craig asked his contacts what was new with them and how they had been faring since the last time they'd talked with him, then he let them guide the topics of conversation.

It took some practice, but once Craig consistently used Right-Side Up thinking, the transformation was dramatic—professionally and personally. Suddenly our sessions together were overflowing with excitement. He literally said, "I can't wait to pick up the phone and start calling people. There's no pressure. It's just fun and very rewarding."

For a moment, I wondered whether it was actually Craig on the phone! But Craig reassured me he was the same guy, just a new, more effective version: "I'm not a people person, but I can do this, and it's great."

Strange as it may seem at first, Craig's newfound confidence came from *outside*, not inside. We have been taught from an early age that self-esteem comes from within. But as you are about to discover in the next chapter, when it comes to consulting, that's a myth.

CHAPTER 2

Building Confidence

How confident are you, right now, about your ability to win substantial new business? Is landing projects as easy as buying candy at the corner store? Or do you sense that winning new business is more like stealing candy from a baby: easy in theory, but you'd feel bad, the tot would probably hold on tighter than you thought possible, and the whole process is terrifying.

Take a moment to rate your business development confidence on a scale of 1 to 10.

HOW CONFIDENT ARE YOU IN
YOUR ABILITY TO WIN BUSINESS?

If you gave yourself a seven or below, you're not alone. Lack of confidence is an incredibly common theme among consultants—and not just for newbies starting out. Recently I was talking with a sixty-two-year-old, highly accomplished consultant who'd been in the business for almost four decades. When I asked her what she most needed to work on to build her practice, she said, "I don't feel confident when I'm talking with people who could use my services."

Wow. If *she's* not confident, is it any surprise you're not either?

Is confidence even important? Of course it is! Sales pros will tell you confidence is critical to making rain, and the research backs them up. Studies at Carnegie Mellon show that people purchasing advice (a.k.a. consulting) tend to choose the more confident source, *even when that source has a poor track record.*

That means if you and some other consultant are each trying to win a project with Yuri Yusimi at Sereus Dough, Inc., the other consultant will win it if he's more confident. You could lose the business even if you're the better consultant!

I doubt this is a revelation to you. You already know confidence is important and you know that sometimes your own is lacking. But, if none of this is new, why isn't your confidence higher?

You're looking for confidence in the wrong place.

Sales pros and self-help gurus alike will tell you to look inside yourself. They say things like, "If you examine your offering and abilities, you'll realize you are worthy. You deserve more clients... so go out there and win them!"

In other words, undertake some deep introspection, get in touch with your immutable, platinum, core worth as a human being, then "fake it 'til you make it." Bluster your way through the insecurities.

Hogwash. That's upside down thinking. Confidence isn't about you. The *lack* of confidence is about you.

IRONICALLY, YOUR SELF-CONFIDENCE
ISSUES STEM FROM THINKING
TOO MUCH ABOUT YOURSELF

The irony of flagging self-confidence is it's an entirely inward-focused phenomenon. We're only bothered by our weak offering, run-of-the-mill abilities, unproven value and shaky sales skills because we're worried about failing. And failing feels bad. To us. Not to Yuri Yusimi, who couldn't care less if we lose a project.

But remember, as we discussed in Chapter 1, your first key to success is Right-Side Up thinking: **it's not about you!**

Stop worrying about yourself, stop judging yourself, stop comparing yourself to others, and stop trying to protect yourself from a bruised ego. When your spirits are down and you focus inwardly, you obsess over your negative traits and bad habits. But when you focus *outwardly*, you will release senseless ballast that's weighing your practice down.

To reiterate: self-confidence is not only important, it's critical. And virtually all independent consultants struggle with their confidence now and again. When you hit one of those rough patches, can you just ignore the problem or wish it away? Of course not. But the solution isn't introspection or bluster.

You boost your self-confidence by reflecting *less* on yourself and more on your targets' problems and aspirations. You'll find your confidence soars when you're on the exact same wavelength as your prospects.

Developing Belief in Your Value

Belief is holding complete faith in your heart and mind that what you're offering is valuable. If you don't believe in your value, your prospects are likely to doubt your worth too. But wait a second; didn't I just say that you shouldn't focus on yourself?

I did. Because your belief in your value as a consultant isn't going to come from you, it's going to come from others. I know plenty of psychologists will take me to task, saying you need to be internally anchored, that you should judge your self-worth by your own internal standards and not some arbitrary bar held up by your parents or society.

But I'm not talking about your worth as a human being. I'm talking about your value as a consultant. And like it or not, *you* do not determine your consulting value.

Prospects and clients—not you—are the arbiters of your value as a consultant!

A Three-Part Confidence Booster

The following exercise uses Right-Side Up thinking to build your confidence. To prepare for the exercise, review actual feedback from past clients. After all, it's *their* opinion that counts. If your folio of feedback is thin, reach out to 10 business contacts you know who could conceivably be purchasers of your consulting services (and who will return your call), and ask for their opinion.

What do they say about your offering, your abilities and, ultimately, the value you provide?

Part 1. Powerful Offering

Is there any evidence that clients have purchased what you offer? A check from a client counts as evidence! If they haven't purchased it from you, then from another consultant? The focus, for now, is not on whether you can close deals but whether you're offering something prospects want to buy.

If there *is* evidence, then you know for a *fact* that your target will purchase what you're offering, provided you communicate it to them the right way at the right time. Therefore, you can believe in the power of your offering. Other things may need work, but at least your offering is valued.

However, if there is no evidence your target wants what you're offering, then skip ahead to the Problemeter exercise in Chapter 5. The Problemeter exercise will help you design your offering to address their needs.

When your practice focuses on those you serve rather than on you, your offering will be solid. You'll know it, see it and believe it.

Part 2. Strong Capabilities

Is there any evidence that you have solved your clients' problem? This is a more emotionally charged question than whether or not your offering is one that clients will purchase. In this part we want to know whether you can deliver the goods.

The uber-important point to remember here is that you're only looking for evidence that you have solved your clients' problem. That's it. Not that you're perfect, or always come up with the "best" answer. Not that you're the most-cited authority in the world at what you do, or better than your competitors, or even "good" at it, whatever that means.

Successful consulting is not about whether you are superior to someone else; it's about whether you can help deliver the results your clients want.

Similarly, you don't have to be successful every time. If you're helping your clients at least 80% of the time, then it's pretty clear you have the wherewithal to deliver on your promises.

Am I condoning mediocre performance and lackluster results? Absolutely not. Always strive to deliver phenomenal value to your clients. But focus on what *clients* see as value—which is an outstanding solution to their problem.

If you can't find any evidence that you have solved your clients' problem or the evidence is very, very shaky, and you still want to stick with your current focus, then I recommend two immediate, remedial actions. Both will make you a better consultant and boost your confidence in yourself:

Take on a pro bono project or two. Get a solid win under your belt. Then you'll have the evidence you need that your skill set is sufficient.

Call other consultants and seek out a subcontracting gig in your area of focus. If you can't point to your own success, then build your chops under the guidance of someone who can.

Part 3. Proven Value

YOUR VALUE IS PROVEN

YES ☐ NO ☐

Finally, we get to the crux of it. Is there any evidence that your clients value what you do? Have you received any appreciative feedback from clients or prospects? Has a client introduced you to someone else (which implies they think you're the bee's knees)?

What about negative feedback? Perhaps a more experienced consultant says you're doing it wrong, or someone posts a negative comment on your blog, or maybe even a project goes sour. Does that evidence cancel out the positive results? No!

Your goal is not to help *everyone* in *every* way *every* time. It's to help *some* people *some* of the time. If you've ever had an appreciative client, then you can rest assured you do add value.

Think of it this way: at one end of the pharmaceutical spectrum are sophisticated, biotech compounds and at the other end is aspirin. Aspirin and similar analgesics may not solve the worst pains. In fact, they may not even work a good portion of the time. Yet, Americans spend $2.6 billion every year on analgesics. That's billions of dollars of value attributed to the most simplistic pain relief that only works a fraction of the time.

Do you really need to solve every client's problem every time to be valuable? Of course not. You could be simple aspirin, and that would be a damn fine thing. If you're a step above that, so much the better.

Plus, over time your success percentage will increase as you become better at your craft and, importantly, better at selecting clients. (Yes, choosing the right clients is one of the secrets to becoming a successful consultant.)

Tim's Story

Tim, a consultant in the upper Midwest, could be the poster child for small business consultants. He looks the part, with the requisite neat suit and tie, intelligent eyes and charming demeanor. When Tim came to me, his business was tepid.

In some ways, Tim was doing everything right. He was actively marketing, and he presented a far more professional image than you'd see from many large firms. His target was a sizeable market that he could easily reach. Yet, interest in his services was lukewarm at best and his confidence was drooping lower than his mustache. As his confidence plunged, so did his list of active clients, creating a vicious circle.

Like most consultants, Tim was determined to solve his confidence problems with upside down thinking. He tried every age-old technique for boosting his self-assurance, and every new age technique too, including some retreats, meditation, and daily affirmations. But none of them improved his business or, ultimately, his belief that he could create the thriving, lucrative consulting practice he desired.

Then he flipped his thinking Right-Side Up. It was like flipping a switch on himself and his business. Instead of worrying about himself and his inner Zen, he started focusing on his clients. Prospects started to take notice, and his business began to surge. Based on client feedback, he realized that hiring and managing young employees was a pervasive, expensive problem in his target market. As a result, he became the regional expert in solving that problem, and now when he talks with prospective clients he's brimming with passion and confidence.

Defeating Negative Self-Talk

I've talked about building confidence and overcoming discouragement, but I know that in some cases those steps and exercises aren't enough to keep our outlook positive and upbeat. Many of us have persistent, personal demons that drag us down into the fiery hell of discouragement, low productivity, self-doubt, or malaise. Like medicine's "superbugs" that resist antibiotics, our demons may have even been made stronger by our failed efforts to dismiss them.

I know this from personal experience. I have wrestled with self-talk that threatened my outlook and my business. When self-doubt was plaguing me, I would hide at my desk all day rather than make new business calls that could surface revenue opportunities.

Then I saw a movie called *A Beautiful Mind* and had an epiphany that allowed me to overcome my demons. I've shared my insight with many of the consultants I've coached over the years, and they've had success with it too.

The movie picks up when Nash, a mathematical genius who won the Nobel Prize in economics moves from Carnegie Mellon University to Princeton to focus on mathematics.

For roughly 90 minutes of the movie we live with Nash, experiencing his rise to success, the joy of meeting and marrying his wife, and also his descent into ruin and despair at the hands of a government agent and scoundrel best friend.

Then (*spoiler alert*), with the same shock Nash must have felt, we discover that many central characters in his life are not real, including the government agent and his best friend. They are products of Nash's undiagnosed schizophrenia.

With the help of medication, Nash recognizes his hallucinations for what they are and prevents them from further directing his actions. He stops interacting with them and resumes a productive, happy life.

In the final scene we see an aged Nash, still a professor, walking the university grounds. He looks to his left, where the imaginary characters stand—completely unchanged by the decades that have passed—then turns back to his path and continues on his way.

And right there, in that final scene, is where I encountered the mental breakthrough that enabled me to banish my negative self-talk. You see, Nash's delusions never fully go away. Scores of years after he has "conquered" his schizophrenia, the characters who plagued Nash are still there, off to the side. But he makes a choice. He chooses not to interact with them.

We can make the same choice. We all suffer from delusions. Virtually everyone has his own, personal set of demons. The key is recognizing them as delusions, understanding that they never fully go away, and, most importantly, choosing not to interact with them.

Like Nash, we can label our delusions and set them aside. When your mind tells you that you're not of value and no one will ever buy consulting services from you, you can recognize it for what it is: a delusion. It sounds real, and it sure feels real, but it's not. And when you know it's just your personal delusions rearing their ugly heads, you can choose to ignore them, and, like Nash, continue on your path to greatness.

Is it easy? Well, it definitely gets easier the more you practice. And don't beat yourself up if you backslide now and again. Just make the choice again to ignore the delusions, knowing that over time your successes will become swifter and longer-lasting.

Now, with confidence built on the solid foundation of Right-Side Up thinking, and negative self-talk evicted to the sidelines, you can win a steady stream of clients. Once you find them, that is. Where, exactly are those clients? As you're about to see, they're closer than you think.

Maximize Impact
(Find Your Killer Offering)

Throughout the early decades of the 20th century, religious leaders delivered fiery sermons. The effects on their congregants were fleeting.

In August 1963 a preacher gave his "I Have a Dream" speech on the steps of the Lincoln Memorial. His nation was forever changed.

Martin Luther King, Jr.'s words were aimed at a single, glaring, national issue, and delivered to hundreds of thousands of sympathetic ears at a moment when the country was clamoring for reform.

If we concentrate on those prospects who will engage with us, and we unwaveringly speak to a challenge plaguing them, we can achieve our most ambitious goals.

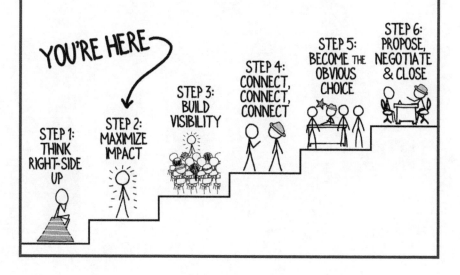

CHAPTER 3

Fish Where the Fish Are

If you're up for making your life easier, raise your hand. (I hope your hand is up.) Okay, put your hand down now, or you won't be able to turn the page. We're about to radically simplify your entire business development challenge. Less work and better results.

The consultants I know who are struggling to land clients are working way too hard and achieving too little. If you're in that boat, there's a darn good chance you're not signing juicy, confidence-building, goal-breaking projects for a very simple reason:

You aren't fishing where the fish are.

It's amazing how straightforward, yet complex, this statement can be. Obviously, we should be selling to clients who want our services, right? So why do so many consultants scrupulously chase an "ideal" client who's elusive and disinterested in their offering instead of pursuing the eager client who is available nearby?

Many consultants anchor themselves to an activity or offering they've completed successfully in the past. Then they cast around, hoping a client is within reach. That's upside down thinking. Are those consultants fishing where the fish are? Probably not. They're just fishing where they happened to moor their boat.

Let's get clear on what "fishing where the fish are" really means. When consulting firms work with me to rapidly grow their client base, I always ask them two questions:

1. *Are your prospects* **aware** *they have the problem you solve?* As often as not, their answer is something along these lines:

   "Some do, but a lot of companies that have the problem don't even realize it. It's actually pretty frustrating."

2. *Do your prospects have an* **urgent** *desire to solve the problem now?* Two very common answers are:

   "No. This is seen as discretionary." and: "They would if they truly understood the consequences. But, no, most of them don't feel they have to solve the problem now."

I arranged the answers to those two questions in a "sexdrant" chart (see Figure 3-1 below). **Prospects who are aware of a need *and* want to solve it immediately are the most likely to hire a consultant**. That's where the money is, and that's why I call targeting that group "fishing where the fish are."

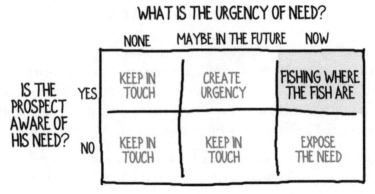

Figure 3-1

You want the bulk of your energy directed toward fishing where the fish are. It's a far easier place to win consulting business. Most consultants are working way too hard because they're *not* fishing where the fish are, and that means one of two things is happening:

1. *They're working on problems that their prospects aren't aware of, and the consultant has to expose the need.* That is what is politely known in our business as a hard sell.

2. *They're sticking to a pond where prospects don't have high urgency. As a result, the consultant has to somehow create that urgency.* That's often an even harder sell!

While it's true that both of those hard sell approaches will yield some business, it is *so* much easier to win business from prospects who are already aware of their problem and urgently want that problem to go away.

I keep talking about problems, but what about aspirations? What if you're more interested in helping clients achieve a higher level of success than in resolving a problem? As long as your prospects are aware of that aspiration and feel an urgent need to achieve it, you're golden. However, projects based on problems are typically easier to close, and since it's clunky to keep talking about problems and aspirations, from now on I'm just going to refer to problems.

Changing Ponds and Reeling in Big Fish

When I started my consulting career, the firm I worked for focused on a narrow specialty within the consumer products world called "trade marketing." Trade marketing deals with the relationship between manufacturers of products like toothpaste and cake mix and retailers like Wal-Mart and Walgreens. My corporate background was perfectly suited for that specialty, which is why I was hired by that particular consulting firm. But a few years into my consulting career, it veered in an unexpected direction.

A friend of mine at a printer manufacturer asked whether we could help him determine what new markets to expand into. Although it was a bit of a left turn from consumer products and retailers, I took on that project, and our work delighted the client.

Shortly after, I won a project with an aerospace company wondering whether they could launch their technologies into new markets. More, similar projects followed—all having to do with expanding into new markets. What did all these clients have in common?

They were aware of an urgent need.

When I co-founded Ascendant Consulting I left the world of trade marketing behind and concentrated on—guess what?—helping companies expand into new markets. I still do that work today for corporations and consulting firms.

IT'S A LOT EASIER TO SELL WHAT PEOPLE WANT TO BUY THAN TO FIND PEOPLE WHO WILL BUY WHAT YOU WANT TO SELL.

VERY GOOD POINT!

Why did I focus my energies on new markets when I had spent years earning my chops in trade marketing? Because of Right-Side Up thinking! My consulting firm's success isn't about me or what I want. *It's about what clients want.* And they were telling me they wanted help getting into new markets. So rather than fish for business in ponds that I knew, I decided to take a more logical and far more successful approach: fish where the fish are. That has made all the difference.

There's a crazy amount of consulting business available. Every year, clients pay advisors over a *trillion* dollars (according to the U.S. Economic Census.) That's a lot of tuna. But most consultants keep working the same pond they've always visited, somehow believing that if they just use a better rod, or practice a better casting technique, or work harder at it, they'll land a better catch.

It's a whole lot easier on your psyche and your bank account if you move to a stocked pond where clients jump at your bait. Does that mean leaving your old comfort zone behind? You bet. Will it be more lucrative? Absolutely!

And don't worry, I'm not suggesting you become an IT consultant if your computer experience consists of calling the help desk, or that you suddenly jump into organizational development if you've never read a book on management.

What I *am* suggesting is that you have more options than you may think. Trade marketing was my old, comfortable fishing hole, and while I could have continued to win business there, I found much richer results in the new-markets pond.

What if You're Fishing Where the Fish Aren't?

I realize not every consultant is willing to change ponds. Besides, what if your fishing hole is generally swarming with hungry prospects, but it's unusually challenging at the moment? What if you already have years of equity built up around the problem you solve, or you employ many consultants who can't easily pivot to a new target and offering?

You can coax prospects into the upper-right box of the sexdrant chart, where you'll reel them in as clients. It's harder work than fishing where the fish are, which is why I always recommend focusing on prospects who are aware of an urgent need.

Let's say Yuri Yusimi at Sereus Dough, Inc. is aware that he needs to increase the throughput of his croissant lines, but he doesn't feel any urgency about addressing the problem. That can be a darn frustrating situation for you, because he'll string you along with promises of a project, but never pull the trigger.

Your three strategies to create urgency are:

1. *Highlight the consequences of inaction.* You could point out that low throughput is robbing Sereus Dough of $1 million in profits every year, and possibly hurting Yusimi's career aspirations.

2. *Compare to benchmarks.* For instance, show a graphic indicating Yusimi's flagging throughput performance compared to Sereus Dough's goals. Comparing Yusimi's performance to other plants might also tap into his competitive spirit and spark action.

3. *Remove roadblocks.* If Yusimi's desire to improve throughput is dampened by his concerns over offending his engineers, you could talk to the engineers and bring Yuri evidence that they're in favor of a project.

Sometimes the need for your services is as plain as day to you, but your prospect is inexplicably blind to the problem. Maybe Yusimi doesn't even realize declining croissant throughput is an issue. Every consultant has met countless prospects who *should* hire him but don't perceive the need.

Your single, highly-effective strategy for exposing need is using a diagnostic. Well-constructed diagnostics come in a variety of forms, but they share two attributes:

1. *Low cost, low risk for the prospect.* A simple quiz, survey, graphic or even a few hours of analysis could be free—a complimentary service you provide to Yusimi. Alternatively, you could offer Yusimi a low-cost assessment of his plant.

2. *The prospect's own evidence convinces him.* Your hypothesis and speculations about throughput are unlikely to move Yusimi. On the other hand, when his plant's data reveal an indisputable, glaring problem, Yusimi will suddenly become a hungry fish.

When a credit union wouldn't move forward on a branding project I had proposed, I pointed out that every month of delay was leaving their customers more confused. I also brought in a project management expert to quell their worries about the complexity involved. Those actions broke the logjam and yielded a signed contract.

What if it's Crowded Where the Fish Are?

A lot of consultants are concerned about competition. What if there are already well-established firms addressing the burning need you'd like to target? That fear may feel even more intense if you're considering a problem that you don't have decades of experience solving, as was the case when I moved from trade marketing to new markets. My answer is pretty simple:

Competition is your friend.

Think about how competitive the fast food industry is. Now think about where fast food enterprises put their restaurant locations. When Mario's Pizza is scouting for a new location, do they seek out a deserted back road where there's no competition? *No!* Just the opposite. They plant themselves at an intersection where there's already a McDonalds, or a KFC, or a Taco Bell, or all three. Why? *Because that's where hungry people are!*

COMPETITION SHOULD BE YOUR FISH-FINDING SONAR. IF THERE'S COMPETITION, THAT'S A GOOD INDICATION YOU'RE ENTERING A FERTILE SPACE.

Is there such a thing as too much competition? Not really. If my math is correct, a trillion dollars in advisory services is enough for you, me and at least three other consultants. Maybe four. Seriously, there is so much business out there that competition shouldn't be your concern.

Right-Side Up thinking applies to your competition too. Consulting isn't about you, and it's not about your competitors either. Consulting is about the clients. If you stop worrying about yourself and your competition and set your sights squarely on where the clients are, you'll enjoy life more and find consulting to be a much easier business.

Plus, in Step 5: Become the Obvious Choice, you're going to learn how to come out on top even when other consultants are in the mix.

The Four Rights

So that's all? Fish where the fish are and you're good to go? Well... no. That's a good start, but it probably feels a bit theoretical. So, let's get practical. It's not enough to simply decide that you'll offer what people need. You have to know specifics. In fact, if you want to open the floodgates and turn a revenue trickle into a stream or even a raging torrent, you need to identify "The Four Rights." The Four Rights are:

1. The *Right* People
2. The *Right* Problem
3. The *Right* Solution
4. The *Right* Time

That's it. *The Right People; the Right Problem; the Right Solution; the Right Time.* Combine The Four Rights and a river of consulting opportunities will start to flow your way.

For most consultants, the Right Time is harder to predict than which Wonka bar holds a golden ticket in *Charlie and the Chocolate Factory.* The reliable countermeasure, of course, was demonstrated by Veruca Salt: the more Wonka bars you open, the higher your likelihood of uncovering a golden ticket.

In other words, since you don't know when—or if—any one, specific, person will become aware of an urgent need you can solve, you eliminate the challenge of identifying the Right Time by stocking your pond with teeming schools of the Right People. Who, exactly, are the Right People? Turn the page to Chapter 4, and let's find out.

CHAPTER 4

The Right People

Getting in front of the Right People is much, much easier than you think—as long as you're thinking in practical, real world terms. On the other hand, it's easy to get caught in the "avatar trap," which is like the candied apple of marketing. (It looks incredibly tasty, but after one bite your teeth will stick together forever and only expensive orthodontia will repair the damage.) Let me quickly explain what the avatar trap is, then give you an approach that will keep your ~~teeth~~ consulting practice healthier.

Have you ever tried, or heard of, the marketing exercise in which you outline your perfect buyer? You're supposed to paint a detailed picture or develop a "persona" or "avatar" of your ideal target. You probably know the drill:

- *What's their position?*
- *What type of company are they in?*
- *Where are they located?*
- *What are their skill sets?*
- *What's their attitude?*
- *What's their hat size?*
- *Do they have their wisdom teeth?*

It can get absurdly in-depth. The theory is that once you've created an avatar of the perfect buyer, you can go out and find people who closely match that image. Nice theory, but it doesn't generate business for a consultant whose revenue is slumping.

Painting a pretty picture of your perfect buyer doesn't magically provoke dream prospects to seek your services. For that matter, they don't start picking up the phone when you call—even if *"they eagerly pick up the phone"* was included in your avatar's definition statement.

That's because the typical description of a perfect buyer is missing the single, absolutely most important attribute. Let's say you define your ideal prospects: *"Forward-thinking vice presidents of operations at fast-growing Fortune 500 companies with headquarters in the Midwest."* Sounds good. But nothing in that description will make a VP of Operations at Caterpillar or Monsanto want to call you or take your call.

What's missing? The first attribute of the Right People is insanely practical: *You can reach them.*

You might argue that you can reach anybody given enough time and dedication. Maybe, maybe not. In the practical world, the Right People are the folks you can engage in conversation quickly.

The quicker you can engage an executive in conversation, the "righter" they are. The time it takes to connect is going to depend on your reputation, how tightly you define the problem you solve (the Right Problem), and how powerful your offering is (the Right Solution). More than anything, though, your ability to reach people depends on how strong your relationship is with them.

That's why the starting point for finding the Right People is looking at your current contact list. These are people you already know. They're prospects who will definitely respond to your phone call or email, not people you *hope* or *think* you can somehow engage in conversation.

Later, in Step 3: Build Visibility, we're going to increase your reach. And that's important, because if the only people who will call you back are family members and entry-level cafeteria workers then, as Tom Hanks (not Jim Lovell) said, "Houston, we have a problem."

But for now, while you're trying to create a surge of revenue, the answer to your prayers is already in your address book.

"Hold on," you say. *"Those people don't buy the types of services I provide."* Great point. In fact, let that point sink in for a moment. If the people you can reach don't buy the services you provide, it's pretty clear why you're not selling more consulting services. So, let me reinforce a comment I made earlier:

It's easier to sell services desired by the people you can reach than it is to find people who desire the services you want to sell.

Hey, wait a second, that sounds suspiciously like... Right-Side Up thinking! When we're thinking about the people we can reach, not ourselves, suddenly they are the perfect target. Almost.

What if the most common desire among the people you can reach is to learn authentic Mesopotamian catchphrases, but your ancient Akkadian is a bit rusty? Or maybe they want a service you offer, but don't want it now. Or what if they're not in a position to write you a check for your advice? Those are fair concerns. That's why the Right People have three other prerequisites in addition to being reachable.

1. Their problem (that you can solve) must be *BIG* enough;

2. Their desire to solve the problem must be *URGENT* enough;

3. Their signing authority must be *HIGH* enough.

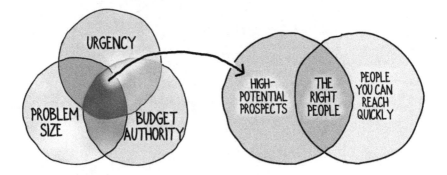

So, we're looking for the *biggest* problems, *highest* urgency, and *largest* budgets, right? Nope. Just big *enough*, urgent *enough*, and high *enough*. The biggest, the highest, and the largest are hard to find. There's only one "biggest" problem, but a gazillion issues that warrant bringing in a consultant like you.

Shouldn't you be chasing CEOs with the proverbial "burning platform"? Prospects like that are a great find. They have money and a huge desire to escape their situation. They're the ticket to high-margin, easy-to-win projects. But finding them can be an exercise in frustration. And frankly, it's not even necessary.

There are plenty of people in your current network who have a big enough problem and enough urgency that they're paying for help.

How do I know this? Because virtually every executive above entry level is responsible for bringing in *someone* to do *something*. Money is spent throughout most organizations.

If your contact list isn't replete with top level executives, don't sweat it. Once a company rises past roughly $100 million in revenue, decisions about bringing in consultants start getting pushed down from the C-suite to subordinates. That's why the CEO isn't a great target anyway.

There's a parallel misconception at work here. It's the belief that we should try to move as high up in an organization as we can. Every salesperson is taught to penetrate an organization up to the C-suite if possible. There are definitely benefits to having contacts at high levels of the organization, but moving higher is actually going in the *wrong* direction!

IF YOU WANT TO WIN MORE CONSULTING BUSINESS FASTER, STAY AT THE *LOWEST* LEVEL OF THE ORGANIZATION THAT HAS SUFFICIENT NEED + URGENCY + BUDGET

The Right People at Sereus Dough, Inc.

For Yuri Yusimi, a plant manager at Sereus Dough Inc., downtime on their plasmatic node machine is a big, urgent problem. But when you reach Yusimi's boss, the VP of manufacturing, that node machine is just one of many issues on the docket, and it's not the most urgent. The COO hasn't even heard of a plasmatic node machine and definitely doesn't care that you can reduce downtime.

Sure, the COO is handing out $500,000 projects while Yusimi's typical project is only $50,000. But you can *win* those $50,000 projects day in and day out, especially if you already know plant managers. Win the projects you can win from the clients you can reach; don't pine after projects you can't win from executives you don't know!

Yusimi meets the Right People criteria: you can reach him and he has sufficient need, urgency, and budget. You don't need to go higher in the organization for this project. In fact, moving higher may slash your likelihood of winning the plasmatic node project.

Keep in mind that during the project you'll meet the VP of manufacturing and perhaps the COO. You'll get to know them and their problems. And maybe the next project you win *will* be the $500,000 operations initiative. Because now the COO fits your Right People criteria: *she's someone you can reach*. Best of all, she's now the lowest level in the organization that has sufficient *need*, *urgency*, and *budget* to do that bigger project.

Okay, you've found the Right People. They're the people you can reach who want you to solve their problem. Obviously, you can't solve *every* problem. You're a consultant, not a handyman. In fact, your most effective business development efforts focus on precisely *one* problem. Which problem, exactly, should you be solving? Let's figure that out next.

CHAPTER 5

The Right Problem

When you're analyzing a client's business, identifying the most insightful question to ask is easier than hitting a grade schooler's piñata. But somehow, when consultants look at their own practice, choosing the best question is more like pinning the tail on the donkey—while practicing pirouettes. For instance, consultants who aren't consistently winning more than $250,000 in annual revenue year typically ask, "How can I reach more buyers?"

But, as you read in Chapter 4, that's the wrong question. Buyers are already right in front of you. They're prospects you already know, and the people you can be introduced to by the people you already know. Instead...

Ask yourself: "What should I talk about with the buyers I can already reach?"

Struggling consultants usually answer that question by looking in the mirror: "What's *my* experience? What are *my* capabilities? What are *my* passions?" That's a natural, normal, understandable place to start. But remember, it's also upside down thinking.

The path to a richer and more rewarding career in consulting is letting Right-Side Up thinking guide you to the Right Problem.

Remember, I wasn't an expert in new markets when I started in consulting. My background was in trade marketing. But prospective clients were telling me that they wanted to know what market to go into and how to penetrate it. They were probably telling me about other problems, too, but getting into new markets was one I knew I could solve or learn to solve. I decided to focus on what *they* wanted.

Rick, a Utah-based consultant, has a similar story. Rick sold medical equipment services to hospitals, and it was a slog. Yet all the time he was selling his services, he overheard hospital executives asking the same questions, such as how much should they pay their doctors? Rick soon realized he could create a system to answer the questions he kept hearing over and over. As a result of Right-Side Up thinking, Rick now sells $2-3 million in consulting services every year without breaking a sweat. *And you can, too.*

Focus

In order to pinpoint your Right Problem, you're going to have to give up the belief that your message should encompass everything—or even a broad range of problems.

It's okay to have broad capabilities, but if you want to be truly successful, the core offering you market needs to be *narrow, narrow, narrow*. Why? Because research shows, unequivocally, that clients look first for experience with their *specific* problem and situation.

To make it into their consideration set, you need to be a specialist, not a generalist.

My friend, Marshall Goldsmith, may be the highest paid executive coach in the world. He earns up to $50,000 per day to advise his clients. If you paid 50 grand for advice, you'd probably listen to it, right? Well, let me pass along the advice that Marshall gives to other coaches and consultants, and treat this as if you've paid $50,000 to hear it:

> *"Have a clear focus, and become the expert at that. Don't get sucked into doing other work every time someone asks if you can do it. I'm an executive coach. I don't do strategic consulting or give how-to speeches. There's nothing wrong with those; they're just not what I do."*

Hold on a second. Couldn't Marshall get big strategy projects if he wanted to? After all, he has every CEO's ear. Yes, he could. But is it wise to dilute his offering? No. Marshall attributes his success to the specificity of his offering and his dedication to providing outstanding advice on a narrow issue (leadership) for a narrow target (CEOs).

You can figure out the Right Problem for your own practice using two powerful, easy to accomplish exercises:

1. Fishing for Problems

2. The Problemeter

Exercise #1. Fishing for Problems

This exercise is going to seem obvious and incredibly intuitive, but most consultants actually make a mistake during the process that creates frustration rather than a full pipeline. To jump into Fishing for Problems, you'll need to make a few phone calls—which, by the way, you could start *today!* First, you call prospects you have any sort of decent relationship with and ask the following question:

> *"What problems have you found so pressing and important that you've actually spent money bringing in outside help to solve them over the past few years?"*

That's the question. Let's say you've known Yuri Yusimi at Sereus Dough, Inc. since you met at the croissant convention years ago. Your conversation sounds like this:

—*mm*—

YOU: "Hi, Yuri."

YURI YUSIMI: "Hi. Good to hear from you..."

At this point you engage in some relationship-nurturing conversation, which depends on the personality of the person you're talking with. Then:

YOU: "Yuri, could I ask you a question? Your insights will be very helpful for me as I try to build my consulting practice."

YURI YUSIMI: "Sure. What's up?"

YOU: "What problems have you or your company found so pressing and important that you actually spent money bringing in an outside resource to help you solve them over the past few years?"

YURI YUSIMI: "Oh. Well, let me think. Do you mean operations problems?"

YOU: "I mean any problems. Was there anything that was pressing and important enough that you brought someone from the outside in to help?"

YURI YUSIMI: "We don't bring in people often. We use an agency, of course, for advertising. And we hired a specialist when we had a plant fire last year..."

—*mm*—

Continue the conversation by asking *"What else?"* until you're right on the edge of being a pest. Don't cross that line, but don't be afraid to probe for more, either.

The Biggest Mistake Consultants Make When Fishing for Problems

The biggest mistake consultants make in the conversation you just read is asking whether clients are interested in their consulting offering, or whether the clients *would* spend money to solve a problem. Those aren't the right questions because they won't give you the answers you need.

Learn what clients have actually spent money on in the past, not what they say they'll do in the future.

Maybe that's not visionary, but it makes money and produces clients. If your contacts hired a consultant to solve their plant efficiency problem in the past, there's a good chance they'll hire someone to address that challenge again in the future. Plus, if you find 20 percent of your contacts have brought in outside help to solve their plant efficiency problem, you can bet another 20 percent will use consultants for the same problem, but haven't yet.

If it's bothering you that you're searching for problems, rather than symptoms, I hear you. Clients use the word "problem" when they're actually seeking help to alleviate symptoms. To keep things simple and stay Right-Side Up, though, I'm lumping symptoms and problems together.

WHAT PROBLEMS HAVE YOU ACTUALLY HIRED A CONSULTANT TO SOLVE?

To make the Fishing for Problems exercise even more effective, also conduct it with your competitors. I've included an outline of this process and a script in an online bonus called, **Fishing for Problems in Other Consulting Firms**.

Exercise #2. The Problemeter

Now we're going to make some magic using a simple spreadsheet, some research, and some educated guessing. It's a seven-step process I call the Problemeter. (After years of study, I've earned a degree in concocting new words.)

Step 1: List the Problems

List all the problems and aspirations you uncovered in the Fishing for Problems exercise and every issue you've been hired to resolve in the past. Don't filter them yet. Just build a big, long list. There's a worksheet for this list I've made available as a download: **The Problemeter Worksheet**.

Step 2: Rate the Pervasiveness

Rate each of the problems as Very High/ High/ Moderate/ Low on a scale of pervasiveness. You're looking to find issues that occur with high frequency across a wide range of clients. A CFO's habit of mumbling financial results to analysts while sucking on lollipops is an issue that might come up once (and is better left to a professional)—you'd rate it low. On the other hand, misaligned goals across departments is a problem every company faces, so you'd rate it very high on pervasiveness.

Step 3: Rate the Urgency

Now scrutinize your list, rating each problem as Very High/ High/ Moderate/ Low on a scale of how urgent the problem or aspiration is when it occurs. In other words, how *strong* is the desire to address the issue relative to other priorities? Global expansion may have moderate urgency; if the prospect's headquarters is on fire, putting it out is going to be at the very top of his priority list.

Step 4: Rate the Expensiveness

Review the list one more time, rating each of the problems as Very High/ High/ Moderate/ Low on how costly it is to leave the problem unaddressed, or to address the issue using internal resources. For example, finding an ice carver proficient in replicating baked goods may be urgent if the annual company picnic is next month, but if it isn't solved, that's not hugely expensive. On the other hand, if an FDA compliance issue is left unresolved, that could cost millions of dollars every day.

Step 5: Sort and Filter

Look for problems and aspirations that are Very High and High across the board. Find the five-to-ten issues that rate highest on pervasiveness, urgency, and expensiveness.

Step 6: Connect to Your Skills

Now rate each of the top problems as Very Strong/ Strong/ Moderate/ Weak, based on your own, personal skills and ability to address the issue. In other words, how likely are you to be able to help clients resolve each issue or achieve each aspiration? *An important note:* This rating is not based on your skill relative to other consultants, but on your skill relative to the clients' needs.

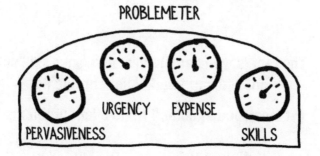

Step 7: Choose Your Right Problem

Scan your list of five-to-ten top issues. Are your skills Very Strong or Strong on any of them? If so, choose the *one* issue that is most pervasive, urgent, and expensive to leave unresolved and where you have strong capability. *That is your Right Problem.*

Laser focus your core offering on one problem that is pervasive, urgent, expensive to leave unresolved, and connects to your skill set.

If you don't have strong skills on *any* pervasive, urgent or expensive issue, then chose one where you think you could build those skills and make a plan to create capabilities. If your only skill is doodling, you can promote that all you want, but you're not going to get consulting gigs. On the other hand, you may find that communicating safety protocols using pictures is a pervasive, urgent, and expensive problem among the people you can reach, and it's a skill you can pick up quickly thanks to your years of idle scribbling.

I hope you noticed that steps 1 through 5 of the Problemeter exercise were all about the clients, not about you—Right-Side Up thinking. Your skill set doesn't come into play until the end. That's because it's the least important part of identifying the problem that will make you a successful consultant.

The fact is, you can always build your skill set, but you can't build client problems.

(At least, you shouldn't build client problems!)

If that feels counterintuitive and scary, don't worry. It feels that way at first to many consultants I work with. But it's so vitally important, it's worth repeating so you can't just skim over it and hope it goes away: *your skill set is the least important part of choosing the Right Problem!*

The Fishing for Problems and Problemeter exercises will help you move from being a vague generalist who doesn't provoke any interest or excitement to a powerhouse problem-solver who focuses on the exact point where clients need help: the Right Problem.

Now you can follow Marshall Goldsmith's advice and become an in-demand, highly paid expert at addressing a specific issue—provided you identify the Right *Solution*. It's a good thing that's next.

BONUS MATERIAL

Bonus Materials available at davidafields.com/winningclients

Fishing for Problems in Other Consulting Firms

The Problemeter Worksheet

CHAPTER 6

The Right Solution

My business school internship was spent at M&M Mars' headquarters, which was conveniently co-located with the M&M's manufacturing plant. Chocaholic heaven, and on mornings when peanuts were roasting, the aroma had employees salivating by the time they walked from the parking lot to the office. You're about to find the consulting equivalent... and it's lower in calories!

What could be better than an offering that is so compelling, so enticing, and so obviously valuable that clients instantly open their wallets the moment they catch wind of it? Nothing. That solution, if you have it, rocks.

The cool thing about consulting, though, is you don't have to have a "killer" solution to be successful. You just have to have the *Right* Solution.

The Role of Breakthroughs and Differentiation in Consulting

A decade or so after my ambrosial days at M&M Mars, I was featured as one of *Advertising Age* magazine's "Marketing Top 100." *Advertising Age* was the bible of the consumer products world, and being recognized among the elite marketers in the country was an incredible honor. Except, those of us behind the scenes knew the success highlighted in the article had little to do with me. I simply had the good fortune to be assigned to, of all things, an incredibly innovative toothbrush developed in Germany and launched in the USA by my predecessor.

That adventure reinforced two lessons every good marketer knows and preaches: 1) breakthrough products will catapult you to success, and 2) the key to winning business is differentiating.

The curious thing is, those two lessons are all wrong for consulting!

Sure, a truly innovative approach can launch a consultant's career into the stratosphere. That's what happened with Eliyahu Goldratt when he developed the Theory of Constraints and wrote *The Goal*, a book that's been consumed by every operations professional since 1984.

But those sorts of breakthroughs roll around once a decade or so. A heck of a lot of consultants have created huge businesses without a breakthrough method or solution.

MOST CLIENTS DON'T WANT A BREAKTHROUGH APPROACH. THEY WANT A RELIABLE SOLUTION.

Similarly, differentiation, the bedrock of every classic marketing plan, has no place in consulting. I frequently receive inquiries from consultants who want help developing a "differentiated positioning that separates the firm from what everyone else is doing." The news I give them is the same as I'll give you:

Consultants should never focus on differentiation.

Differentiation is *not* what sells consulting business. In fact, I've seen consultants consistently lose business—good business they could have won—by striving to differentiate their firms. *"But don't I have to show buyers how I'm different from all the other firms that do what I do?"* is the question I commonly hear when we get into this topic. The answer is, yes, and no.

Yes, you need a reason for decision makers to choose you, but no, it's not the reason you think.

In fact, in the rare instances where a decision maker asks, *"Why should I use you rather than Cheapo Consulting or Big-Name Associates?"* there's only one answer. I'll give you that answer in a moment, but first, it's important to understand why differentiation works for consumer products, and why it's practically anathema for consulting.

Consulting is Not Like Consumer Products!

When a consumer approaches the supermarket shelf, she believes the products will fulfill on their basic promise. All toothpastes prevent cavities. As a result, marketers try to win over the shopper by suggesting their brand will make her mouth feel tingly, or help her gums heal, or make her more kissable. (Definitely more kissable.)

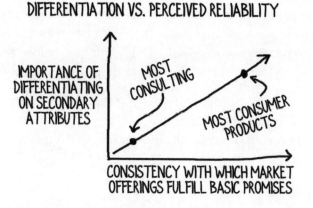

DIFFERENTIATION VS. PERCEIVED RELIABILITY

IMPORTANCE OF DIFFERENTIATING ON SECONDARY ATTRIBUTES

MOST CONSULTING

MOST CONSUMER PRODUCTS

CONSISTENCY WITH WHICH MARKET OFFERINGS FULFILL BASIC PROMISES

When a decision maker on a project approaches a consulting firm, however, she does *not* believe most firms will fulfill on their basic promise.

Why? Because every executive has seen consulting projects fail or has been severely disappointed with a consultant. The archives of tens of thousands of companies are bursting with thick, expensive consulting reports that looked and sounded good when they were delivered, but didn't pan out, or were never implemented.

They're expensive mistakes that make buyers more than a little gun-shy when it comes to hiring another consultant, which is why buyers of consulting services *aren't* looking for *different*; **they're looking for a solution they can rely on.**

So, the next time an executive asks you why he should hire you rather than the competition, your conversation should sound like this:

—*mm*—

YURI YUSIMI: "Why should I hire you rather than Cheapo Consulting, or Big Name Associates?'

YOU: "Because working with us will give you the highest likelihood of achieving your goal, and the least chance of something going wrong that could hurt you or the business."

—*mm*—

Now, you may be thinking that the *follow-up* to that answer has to show how different and uber-smart you are. Again, yes and no. Yes, you need an approach that helps the client believe you will achieve the goal. What that should look like is explained below. But no, presenting yourself as different, per se, is not as important as you think.

The work you'll be doing in Steps 3-5 (Building Visibility, Connecting, and Becoming the Obvious Choice) will make it so apparent you're the consultant they should retain, that you won't need to be "different."

What *is* the Right Solution?

The Right Solution—the core offering your prospects will quickly sign on the dotted line to acquire—is one that meets the following four criteria:

- Simple
- Easily communicated
- Highly relevant
- Efficient

The Right Solution is astonishingly straightforward. I don't know exactly what that solution is for your practice because every narrow field and niche is different, but I do know the client will have the same reaction to it, no matter what it is you do: "That's surprisingly simple."

At which point you'll reply, *"Yes, it is simple. But it's not easy."*

Clients get that. They want that. Executives are far more likely to buy a solution they understand than one that seems mystifyingly complex, difficult to grasp or shrouded in mystery. They intuitively adopt Occam's razor: *the simplest explanation is usually the correct one.*

Hand in hand with simplicity is making sure your solution is easy to communicate. You don't want to get all tongue tied and flustered when you explain your approach. Beyond that, your prospect is more likely to stick with a solution that he can quickly and reliably explain to his peers than one that positions him to make vague, trust-me statements like, "Well, I don't totally understand what they do, but they seem to have a good track record."

You don't have to reveal every detail about how you do your work, though, honestly, it's okay if you do. The best solutions are totally understood by your clients. If you can use a graphic or mnemonic or two-line case study to make your offering more memorable, so much the better.

Remember, just because a client understands what you do, doesn't mean they can actually *do* what you do. That's why they hire you. I know that if my car won't start, there are only two possible problems: the fuel system or the electric system. But knowing those facts doesn't make me a mechanic.

The Right Solution is also highly relevant; i.e., it's focused squarely on delivering results for the prospect's specific problem or aspiration. You spent considerable time identifying that specific issue in Chapter 5. Keep Right-Side Up thinking firmly in mind, though: once you identify your core offering, you may need to tweak it (or abandon it) for different prospects. The Right Solution for each prospect has to be highly relevant to his unique situation and need.

Finally, the Right Solution is efficient, meaning you can deliver it reliably and with high margins as more and more clients request your prowess. Leverage, systemization, and efficient delivery infrastructures are outside the scope of this book. However, as you're identifying your Right Solution, keep in mind that you must be able to make good on your promises and make a healthy profit along the way.

You may have started this chapter thinking I would lead you to a fancy, sophisticated, breakthrough offering. I didn't because you don't need that any more than M&M Mars needed a scent more sophisticated than roasting peanuts to trigger a salivary response. Just solve the client's problem. *Simple, easily communicated, relevant, efficient.* That's it. *THAT* is the Right Solution.

You've identified your narrow target, chosen the pervasive, urgent, expensive problem your clients want to solve, and cooked up a dynamite solution. You're ready to stock your pipeline. Now it's time to pull these elements together into a high-impact, memorable description that you can use to snag clients. To do that you'll need a Fishing Line.

CHAPTER 7

The Fishing Line

You've identified the Right People, the Right Problem, and the Right Solution. Now let's use that combination to get some prospects on the hook. If you poke around books on rainmaking and professional service sales, you'll find that business development is often portrayed as "hunting." But hunting is the wrong metaphor.

Independent consultants who approach business development that way get frustrated and go hungry because attracting consulting clients is like fishing, not hunting. We want to hook our clients, not shoot them.

Sometimes our target will grab the hook right away, and we'll quickly land a healthy project. Other times a prospect will circle the hook, swim away for a while, then come back and grab it. And yet other times, if we construct an enticing enough lure, fish who see

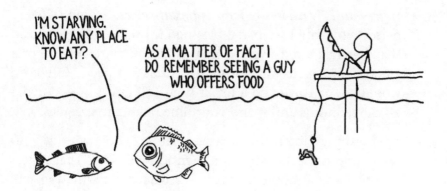

it will tell their struggling friends about our hook, and suddenly prospects will appear as if from nowhere—without even moving we'll be fishing where the fish are.

Just when you think a metaphor has been taken to its limit, there's more: If you want to be a great angler, you need a strong Fishing Line.

Your Fishing Line

Your Fishing Line is a ten-to-fifteen word statement that succinctly, precisely describes your target and the issue you address (a problem or aspiration). Your Fishing Line does *not* include your solution. Hold that in reserve—sort of like the net that allows you to scoop the fish up once you've reeled it in.

A powerful Fishing Line works for you in multiple ways:

- *It's easy for you to remember.* It rolls off your tongue, even when you're flustered, and believe me, every consultant gets flustered or tongue-tied occasionally when face to face with a potential client.

- *It's easy for your prospects to remember.* That means even if Yuri Yusimi at Sereus Dough, Inc. doesn't need you right now, when the right time comes along, you'll be the person he calls. Brrrng, brrrng, your phone starts ringing when your Fishing Line sticks in people's minds.

- *It very quickly allows prospects to self-select.* Imagine if every person you could see had a blazing LED sign on his forehead that signaled a red "No!" if he wasn't a potential client, or a green "Yes!" if he was a high-potential prospect. Holy cow, wouldn't that save you a lot of time and effort? You'd avoid all the redheads and spend your time talking to greenies.

  Your Fishing Line is the next best thing. People who fit your target and have the issue you mention will say, "That's me!" and those who don't fit your target/issue combination will either say, "That's not me!" or their eyes will glaze over. Either way, you've saved a lot of time and effort.

- *It's easy for your prospects to repeat to others correctly.* Most consultants dream of other people doing their selling for them. Well, that dream can only come true for you if other people can quickly and easily say what you do. From what I've seen, if it takes you five minutes (or even 30 seconds) to describe your place in the world, no one else will be passing along your name.

A short phrase that describes the target market and precise issue. Sounds simple, right? It's surprisingly difficult. In fact, 98 percent of consultants don't have a good Fishing Line. Last week I was working with a boutique consultancy on the East Coast. One rainmaker was landing millions of dollars of business on the strength of his personality alone, but the rest of the firm's partners rarely landed a client. When I asked what was holding them back they told me they didn't have a simple way to describe what their firm does. That's incredibly common, and you may have felt that way too.

Warning: A Fishing Line is *NOT* an Elevator Pitch

The majority of consultants are looking for a compelling, thirty-second commercial that will magically turn complete strangers into eager prospects. In other words, the proverbial elevator pitch. I don't believe in elevator pitches for two reasons:

1. *Consultants don't pitch.* Pitching is talking at someone with the message, "Please give me what I want. Along the way,

you'll benefit." That's not what we do. In fact, as consultants we do the exact opposite. We *inquire and listen* and our message is, "I'd like to help you achieve what you want. Along the way, I'll benefit."

2. *Consulting business isn't won in thirty seconds.* That's a hunting mentality and I don't care how good your commercial is, that's not how consulting is sold. By and large, this is a trust and relationship business. We're solving complex, expensive problems linked to an emotional impact. That makes for a longer sale.

A Fishing Line doesn't take 30 seconds and it's not meant to win business. If your Fishing Line isn't meant to win business, what is it meant to do? That's easy. Create conversations.

Thirty-second pitches don't create consulting projects, but conversations do. You toss your Fishing Line out into the world, over and over again, to *hook* potential clients. When your Fishing Line prompts Yuri Yusimi to say, "That's interesting, tell me more," it's worked perfectly. Do *not* fall into the trap of thinking your Fishing Line is supposed to win business.

Constructing a Powerful Fishing Line

A great Fishing Line can take years to perfect, although you can create a serviceable version in about half an hour. The key is to communicate the two parts of the Fishing Line—your narrow target and the tightly-defined issue you address—in fewer than 15 words.

The more precise your target, the better. The more concrete the issue, the better. The shorter the better. You might think it's hard to be super precise about your target and issue in only a few words. You'd be correct. That's why it will take time, effort, many iterations, and some trial and error. When you finally get it, though, you'll know it. Let me give you a couple of successful Fishing Lines.

Some Effective Fishing Lines

One Australia-based consultant I coached tells prospects:

> *"I work with IT companies that are underperforming in the Asia-Pacific region."*

That's an absolutely crystal clear Fishing Line, and it's incredibly effective. Could the target be narrower? Sure, but the balance between precision and brevity is perfect.

The Fishing Line for Ascendant Consulting (my firm) is:

> *"I work with B2B manufacturers who are tired of slugging it out for market share."*

Fifteen words that precisely identify the target and the issue they're facing. If I'm talking to a marketing executive at a B2B (business to business) manufacturer and he hears that Fishing Line, I can tell you from personal experience he'll be hooked. He'll want to know everything about how I can guide him into new, less competitive markets.

For my work with consulting firms, my Fishing Line is:

> *"I work with boutique consultancies who want to win more projects from more clients at higher fees."*

Very narrow target (not professional service firms in general, for example) and very precise aspiration. Yes, I exceeded the fifteen word guideline, but the "more, more, more" cadence is easy to remember.

How to Recognize a Weak Fishing Line

As I mentioned, developing a powerful Fishing Line is much harder than it first appears. My guess is yours needs some work. Use the Common Fishing Line Mistakes Checklist below to diagnose weak spots and improve your Fishing Line:

Common Fishing Line Mistakes Checklist ✎

☐ **No problem.** If your Fishing Line doesn't state a concrete problem (or aspiration) in the client's language, it's like using jute thread instead of twenty-pound nylon. Solutions and outcomes are not problems! "We get rid of bugs" is a solution. "We help homeowners whose kitchens are infested with roaches" is a Fishing Line.

☐ **Too broad a problem.** "I help companies grow" sounds to prospects like, "I'm a generic consultant who has no special skills or expertise you need." Near my office is a business named "Mr. Shower Door." I bet he wins a lot of business from people who need shower doors. Why? Because people know he solves exactly their problem.

☐ **Too many problems or targets.** Every "and" in your Fishing Line cuts the power in half. "I work with financial services and insurance companies..." is half as powerful as working with one target or the other. You may think you're doubling your

I WORK WITH OPERATIONS AND REGULATORY
EXECUTIVES IN THE INSURANCE, BAKERY, AND...

UH, WHAT WAS THAT
FIRST ONE AGAIN?

pool of prospective clients, but in fact you're halving the like-lihood that any prospect thinks you specialize in *his* needs. Every "and" also torpedoes the memorability of your Fishing Line. People don't remember multiple ideas very well.

☐ **Too long.** After 15 words the power starts to fall off; after 20 words the usefulness plummets. If your Fishing Line is too long it won't be memorable or understandable.

☐ **Too broad a target.** "Companies" and "Executives" are two popular choices that have no value at all. Who *isn't* an exec-utive at a company? If your words don't exclude most people, they're not adding power to your Fishing Line.

☐ **Too approach-oriented.** Consultants *love* to talk about their approach. We are convinced that we need to lead with our outstanding methods. It sounds like, "I help leadership teams achieve clarity by unifying their mission and yada yada yada..." That started as a good Fishing Line then took a nose dive. Prospects don't care *how* you do something ("by unifying their mission...") until they've determined that *what* you do is relevant. Your Fishing Line is all about rele-vance. Leave it at *"I help leadership teams achieve clarity"* and people will remember it and inquire when their leadership team is in murky waters.

☐ **Too much justification.** The other siren song to consultants is justifications for why a prospect should work with us. "We have 20 years of experience working with advertisers." Hmm. The target is vague ("advertisers"), the problem is nonexistent and the focus is upside down and irrelevant.

Exercise: Construct and Test Your Fishing Line

Now that you know how to construct a powerful Fishing Line and how to recognize some of the most common issues, take 15 minutes to develop at least ten possible Fishing Lines for your consultancy. Once you have ten, choose the three you like best and try them out with prospects and contacts over the next three months. You'll quickly learn which ones generate no interest and which ones have promise.

Over time you'll tweak and fine tune the most promising Fishing Line into the set of words that will carry your consulting firm to the next level of success. Don't be alarmed if it takes you a while. I worked with that consultant in Australia for 18 months before her Fishing Line emerged. In retrospect, your Fishing Line will seem obvious. And that's exactly what you're ~~shooting~~ fishing for.

If tossing your Fishing Line out over and over again sounds exhausting, I bet you'd prefer that clients just jumped into your boat unbidden. That'd be nice, right? That's not only nice, it can also be your reality if enough prospects think of you as a resource that can help them. But how do you create that kind of awareness without spending a fortune on advertising and promotion? You leap onto Step 3: Build Visibility.

Build Visibility

(Become Known by Your Prospects)

Winston Groom's delightful novel about an idiot savant sold 30,000 copies. It was his most successful book. He's virtually unknown, though.

The movie version of Groom's work has entranced over 200 million people. The director and actors are constantly sought-after and paid princely sums. You've undoubtedly seen Forrest Gump.

—

A striking idea, innovative solution, or breakthrough approach may earn you moderate success.

Move into the limelight where prospects can't help but notice you. Now you're positioned for financial freedom.

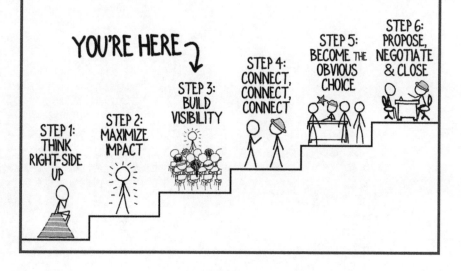

CHAPTER 8

Building Visibility

Many independent consultants want to build their business SOLELY through word-of-mouth, by which they really mean referrals. The word they should have in their mouths is "marketing." Despite the disdain with which many consultants view it, marketing is not a four-letter word. (I know you're blown away by my letter-counting prowess.)

Sure, I know a number of practitioners who have built successful firms purely on word-of-mouth. They built their reputations organically, over time. No marketing required. They are the fortunate few.

The rest of us need to get out there and become visible to the people who can help us grow our practices. If we want business from Yuri Yusimi at Sereus Dough, Inc., we need to wave our arms with Michael Jackson glitter gloves on to catch his eye, then impress him with our bakery-themed pop songs.

But wait! Don't pass Go, don't collect $200, and don't even *think* about marketing, or what it feels like to be in the spotlight, before you step back and ponder this Consulting Truth:

Most struggling consultants don't have a VISIBILITY problem, they have an IMPACT problem.

If your pipeline is woefully thin, it's natural to think that you need to be talking to more decision makers. That's true, except there's no point in getting in front of multitudes of executives if your message has all the sticking power of dry spaghetti.

That's why it's critical you make sure you've nailed Step 2: Maximize Impact before you jump into Step 3: Build Visibility.

After all, using your glitter gloves to attract a passing glance doesn't accomplish much. Targets only turn into prospects when they think of you as a resource to help them with a specific issue. Hence the bakery songs. It's easy to confuse visibility with exposure. But they're not the same.

Exposure is just getting your name out into the world. It's waving your arms around. Visibility, on the other hand, occurs when prospects start to pay attention.

Visibility: Relevant, High-Value Exposure

To become highly visible, you need exposure (of course), but you also need to be perceived as relevant and a source of value.

You already know how to be relevant, because that was the whole point of Step 2: Maximize Impact. It boils down to focusing on a narrow target and a tightly-defined problem. Clients rarely buy the services from independent consultants that are generalists. On the other hand, executives pay handsomely for specialists whose narrow Fishing Line precisely matches the problem they urgently need to solve. A couple of examples:

- I know a consultant in Southern California who writes, speaks and offers advice solely related to a complex polymers issue. Business flows into him every day from a wide range of prospects who have very little in common other than they all have a technical challenge with polymers. Because that consultant addresses an extremely narrow issue, his target can be wide, and his paycheck is even wider.

- Another consulting firm I work with only targets municipal departments of sanitation in California. That's a pretty darn narrow target! As a result, they successfully sell millions of dollars of projects that address a handful of issues.

Unfortunately, I also know hundreds of independent consultants whose target is "Companies over $50 million" or "VPs of Marketing." No specificity at all. They tell their prospects they focus on general, generic problems like, "Helping you get unstuck" or, "Achieving faster growth." The result is low relevance, low appeal, low visibility… and low revenue. Your focused Fishing Line will make you relevant.

Fortunately, you can knock off the other two parts of visibility— exposure and high-value—simultaneously with strong marketing. When your marketing is built on Right-Side Up thinking, you're highlighting topics and issues your target is looking for, where he looks for it, in language he understands.

That's pretty high-level, though. Let's get practical and concrete. Are there specific exposure-enhancing, visibility-building, powerhouse marketing tactics that are best for attracting more clients? You bet!

Your Visibility-Building Toolkit: The Five Marketing Musts

Based on my work with consulting firms across a wide range of disciplines, I've found Five Marketing Musts that are the backbone of increasing your visibility. They are:

- Writing
- Speaking
- Trade Associations
- Digital Presence
- Networking

All of these marketing tools can be effective, and all can simultaneously increase your exposure and your stature as a high-value resource. If none of them feels like your cup of tea, or you're resisting the idea of doing any visibility-building, you're going to find yourself in a world of financial hurt.

Consultants who start their firms with a solid roster of clients based on their previous employer and close colleagues often think winning new projects is easy and will remain easy. It is, and it won't. Those consultants invariably hit a wall at the five-to-seven-year mark.

Every consultant needs to engage in at least *two* of the Five Marketing Musts. Which of the five you prioritize depends on a single factor: what you will actually tackle consistently. If the notion of being in the spotlight on stage turns your legs to jelly then don't make speaking your first priority. If penning 250 words is less appealing than trimming your aunt's toenails, pick one of the other marketing vehicles.

Which are right for you, and how do you go about making it all happen? You'll find the answers you need in the next few chapters. Of course, there's no injunction against layering any other marketing tactics on top of the Five Marketing Musts.

What if Nothing is Working?

Visibility-building takes time. For most consultants, your pipeline is a reflection of the business-development work you did six-to-nine months ago. So, what do you do if you have absolutely no projects or prospects, and your marketing doesn't seem to be getting traction quickly? Supplement your marketing with "Bread & Butter" projects from two sources:

1. Pro bono
2. Subcontracting

Work begets work. As I mentioned in Chapter 2, your confidence will shoot up dramatically when you're actively helping a client—even an unpaid client—solve the issue you're trying to become known for. In the very early days of my consulting firm I took on a pro bono organization design project for a local congregation. Their enthusiasm over the work I delivered gave me the confidence and reputation boost I needed to jump-start my practice.

How Much Time?

One of the most frequent questions I'm asked is how much time you should devote to marketing and building visibility. If you aren't overloaded with clients and projects, the answer is easy: every free moment. If you're swamped with work, the answer is still easy: carve out at least 20 percent of your time for acquiring new clients.

Treat business development the way you'd treat a client who promised you lifetime shipments of Belgian truffles: with slavish devotion and unwavering commitment. Over the years, new business will be your most consistent, best-paying source of revenue.

WHERE TO SPEND YOUR TIME

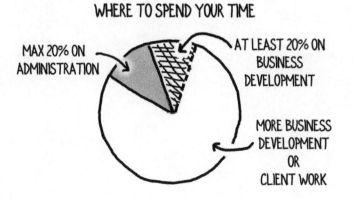

Whether you have one day a week to devote to your marketing, or you're currently "sans clients," it's time to get your visibility-building up and running. Since writing is going to be an important part of the mix for most consultants, let's start there.

CHAPTER 9

Writing

Want to create a steadier stream of clients for years to come? Then pick up your pen, crayon or keyboard, turn to a blank page and start writing. The marketing power of writing is undeniable. It's easier to reach a large audience (i.e., get exposure) with writing than with speaking, networking, or working with trade associations. And with the help of your digital presence (the fourth Marketing Must) you can get your name and message in front of thousands of prospects within a couple of days.

Good writing greases the skids for every other type of marketing: attracting speaking gigs, giving you an easy entrée for networking, magnifying your value to trade associations, and boosting your findability online.

Writing also bequeaths an enduring, cumulative benefit to your business. Over the years, your body of work will grow, reinforcing your reputation as an expert, supporting your digital presence, and nurturing your relationship with prospects—even without a personal touch.

What to Write

You have limited time to knock out some marketing, and writing can definitely swallow a barrel of minutes before anything useful emerges. Given that, should you direct your energy to newsletters, or a book, or something else?

Figure 9-1 arranges the most common formats on two dimensions: the vertical axis depicts the Visibility power (relevance, reputation-value, and exposure), while the horizontal axis shows the Time (to write and disseminate). I've circled the vehicles I recommend most.

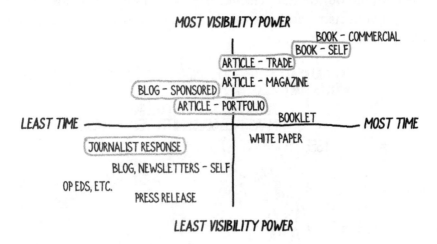

Figure 9-1

With only a few minutes at your disposal, the best combination of quick and impactful is responding to journalists' queries. In two minutes you can shoot off a response that will earn you a quote in a journal or on a website your prospects visit. That mention may even serve as a foot in the door to write your own article for the journal or website that featured you.

The two best sources of queries are PR Leads and HARO. I've subscribed to both for years. I've also found the formula for great responses to journalists that works over 80 percent of the time:

1. *Think Right-Side Up.* Put yourself in the reporter's shoes. What do they want?

2. *Write a catchy headline.* Even a two sentence response warrants a headline.

3. *Offer a short, quotable point.* Three sentences at most that fit the writer's story without editing.

What they *don't* need is a long, rambling explication of your theories. Nor do they need pages of your credentials, a statement that promotes you or some off-topic proclamation—no matter how interesting it is to you.

Here's an example of a response I wrote to a journalist that posted a query about training retail employees to sell:

―ᴍᴍ―

MY HEADLINE: The Best Salespeople Aren't Salespeople.

MY TEXT: Training your employees to sell is a losing proposition, and not just because training of any kind has proven to be largely ineffective (versus coaching, which works). The winners at retail aren't salespeople. They're purveyors of a compelling experience.

―ᴍᴍ―

That response generated an interview and a citation as an expert in the journalist's article.

Articles and Blog Posts

If you're up for writing more than two minutes at a stretch, the next best vehicles are blogs and articles. Both vehicles can be published or distributed by you (i.e., part of your portfolio) or by a supporter such as a general magazine (e.g., Inc. or Forbes), a trade magazine (e.g., Waste News), or a trade association. The best bang for your buck comes from narrowly focused supporters such as trade magazines.

If you're a bakery operations specialist, for example, you're going to pick up far more prospects from *Modern Dough-Twister Monthly* (whose readers are hungrily searching for solutions to their flaky problems) than you will from millions of browsers of *Good Housekeeping.*

Don, the managing partner at a firm I work with on the East Coast, regularly pens articles very specific to compensation issues. His articles have limited distribution, yet they reach his target. As a result, he gets two-to-three inquiries a week from prospective clients.

For quite a number of years I contributed a monthly column to *Industry Week*, and that not only produced awareness, it also helped me craft the content for my first book and for speeches. (If you're interested in writing regularly for a trade journal, you may want to download this bonus resource: **How to Land Your Own Column in Eight Easy Steps.**)

The subject of your writing can be everything and anything that's Right-Side Up; i.e., topics deeply relevant to the prospects you're targeting. (Not upside down pieces promoting yourself!) Any time a prospect asks you for advice, they're also suggesting the topic for an article.

At the top of the heap in terms of visibility power and time required are books. Writing and publishing a good book will take you months or years of effort, but it's worth it. Nothing shouts *"This person's an authority"* as loudly as a book. Commercially published books often hold more weight than self-published works, but if you can't obtain a publishing contract or traditional publishers' lengthy, unsupportive process isn't your cup of tea, self-publishing may be for you. I've seen both routes work for consultants.

Five Quick Writing Tips

- *Pile on the examples and stories*. Don't let your writing drift off into dim lands of concept and theory. Punctuate your ideas with colorful, real-world applications.

- *Write compelling and interesting vs. different and new*. Don't struggle to find something novel to say. Clients would rather hear an old, proven idea conveyed in an intriguing, memorable way than hear an entirely new idea. My goal for prospects' reactions to my writing is 80 percent "I knew that" and 20 percent "That's new." If the balance of unexpected information creeps much higher, then readers will start to trust you less.

- *Make your writing actionable*. Have a point. What should readers do next? Along those lines, make it easy for that next action to be to contact you. Ensure your phone number and email address are easily found on everything you write.

- *Edit*. Michael, a dear friend of mine who was an avid student of writing, never tired of reminding me, "There's no such thing as great writing. Only great rewriting." If you're not a great editor (and few people edit their own work well), enlist someone to edit and proof your work.

- *Be prolific*. Write often. Rarely does a single article, blog post, or newsletter instantly create business. Even your commercially published book may not quickly generate clients. Writing builds over time, and quality emerges from quantity.

Protecting Your Intellectual Property (IP)

How much of your "secret sauce" should you reveal in your articles and speeches? You've spent years developing your ideas and approaches and you don't want competitors to snap them up in a few minutes. Also, if you offer all the answers in an article, clients won't need you. Right?

Wrong. Obviously, plagiarism isn't acceptable and you're within your rights to combat wholesale theft of your IP. But overall, just don't sweat it. First, there's enough consulting business for you to build a profitable practice, even if your competitors "steal" your ideas.

Second, when people other than you are promoting your ideas, the ideas become more credible. You don't want to be the *only* person talking about the benefits of daily chocolate on productivity. More buzz is better for your business.

And, as the *originator* of the theory everyone's talking about, you're the one with the most experience. You'll be the consultant clients seek. (By the way, if chocolate turns out to boost productivity, you read it here first.)

Finally, if Yuri Yusimi can solve his bakery problem by merely reading an article or buying a book, do you really think he's going to spend $50,000 or $500,000 hiring you? Of course not. No amount of content you reveal can chase away a big consulting gig. In fact, the opposite is true. The more you give, the more Yusimi will realize you're an expert and want your expertise applied first hand at Sereus Dough, Inc.

There's no question that your writing, over time, will boost your visibility and attract prospects. Plus, there's another benefit: writing is the most common path to winning speaking gigs. And, as you're about to see, once you land a speaking gig, you're on the fast track to new clients.

BONUS MATERIAL

Bonus Materials available at davidafields.com/winningclients

How to Land Your Own Column in Eight Easy Steps

CHAPTER 10

Speaking

If writing isn't your thing, don't despair. I know a very successful consultant who has trouble putting two words together on paper, but put him in front of an audience and the words flow like honey, and clients are drawn in like bees. Or bears. (Neither sounds comfortable, but you get the idea.)

Speaking in front of an audience is the fastest, most reliable path to winning new business, provided you have the right speaking gig. Standing on an apple crate in the middle of Times Square may garner you plenty of exposure, but you're not likely to win a client. On the other hand, when you're in front of a room full of high-potential prospects, speaking is an express train to revenue growth.

Every speech you make to an audience of more than twenty prospects in your target market should yield at least one new client, and I'm going to show you exactly how to make that work.

Speaking allows you to become instantly known by dozens or hundreds of captive prospects. They'll listen to you and absorb your message quicker than a dry sponge tossed in a pot of soup—a feat that's difficult to replicate even with a well-written book. (I don't recommend throwing books into soup.)

Plus, if you let your personality shine through, your audience will connect with you on a personal level and like you. To make that connection, it's crucial to be yourself when you're in the spotlight. Some speakers are dynamic storytellers, and that works for them. My style is very conversational and that works well for me. Your natural personality is going to work best for you, with a couple of caveats:

First, you can't be Marla Milquetoast on stage even if you're naturally timid and shy. Speak with energy and passion, and your audience will respond to you in kind. Second, even though you're the expert up on stage, avoid becoming Professor Know-It-All. No one likes to be talked down to.

Just be yourself. The mere fact that you're holding the microphone and speaking with some degree of eloquence instantly confers authority status on you. And that builds trust.

If speaking is a new venture for you, I recommend practicing and perfecting your speaking style while getting friendly, professional feedback. A free speech or two at the local library, or even presenting in front of a few colleagues will help you build your chops.

A well-crafted speech can uncover needs, spark wants and illustrate the value of solving the problem you address. Voila, you have covered *Know*, *Like*, *Trust*, *Need*, *Want* and *Value* in about an hour. Get those Six Pillars of Consulting Success working for you and boom, new clients will be knocking on your door. (We'll delve deeper into the six pillars in Chapter 17.)

Where to Speak

If you're very clear about the problem you solve, and that problem is pervasive, urgent and expensive to leave unresolved (see the Problemeter exercise in Chapter 5), I can guarantee your speeches will be attended by decision-making executives who want to hear your message.

The best venues are typically meetings hosted by trade and industry associations and magazines. A speech in front of the right industry group will garner more speeches from related groups and highly lucrative internal gigs at corporate meetings.

General audiences, like the local Kiwanis and Rotary clubs, are much easier to secure and they're excellent for practicing your material. In general, it's unlikely you'll find clients at civic organizations, but you may get lucky and find that Lenny Local, who attends Rotary meetings, is also an influencer at the Intergalactic Bakery Association, where you'd like to speak.

Self-hosted events can be very effective, though they require considerable effort to coordinate. A self-hosted event is a breakfast meeting, lunch-n-learn, cocktails session, executive roundtable, or even an entire conference that you put together and invite prospects to attend.

The great part is you know you'll get the gig. The downside is the upfront investment of time and money. Your ROI from a self-hosted event directly reflects your ability to easily attract a large audience of prospects.

How to Win Speaking Gigs

Do you want to know the secret to winning a speaking gig? *You must have a killer title.* No matter how good or bad your actual content is and no matter what type of venue you're shooting for, the speech title is your winning (or losing) ticket.

A great speech title is provocative, obvious, and tweaks a burning issue you know is on your prospects' minds. Coming up with a killer speech title will take some time and effort. It's not a five-minute exercise. Bad titles will torpedo your odds of winning a gig. They sound like the following:

- "How to Inspire Your Managers"
- "Ten Tips for Becoming a More Profitable Company"
- "The Secret to Operational Effectiveness"
- "Emerging Uses of Interplasmatic Reference Points in Post Production Waste Processing"

Actually, that last one might be a killer title if your audience is all lathered up about post-production waste processing, and interplasmatic reference points are the sexiest new development. But I can assure you, the first three titles are a step below snooze land.

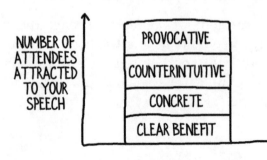

BUILDING A KILLER TITLE

One of the consulting firms I work with is headed by a veterinarian. After a little bit of prodding and a whole lot of mental elbow grease, she came up with the following title: *"Death in a Can: Why Your Pet Food is Killing Your Pets."* It took about six seconds for her to win a speaking gig from her target, the biggest association of pet food manufacturers. *That's* a provocative title. It's obvious what she's talking about, and it tweaks a major sore point for pet food makers.

Once you have a killer topic, there are five paths to take from your comfy office chair to the big stage:

1. ***Respond to calls for speakers***. Most associations issue a call for speakers six-to-nine months before their next conference. Sometimes there's more advance notice, sometimes less. Submit your killer topic along with a pithy write-up and you'll generate some interest. Don't *only* rely on this approach because the competition is insanely stiff and even a killer title may not win you a spot on stage.

2. ***Leverage writing relationships***. One of the easiest and most effective ways to win a speaking gig is to ask the editor of a trade journal you've been writing for to connect you with their event organizer.

3. ***Progress from local to national***. The surest path to a speaking gig when you're not well known is by way of relationships at the local level. Leverage your current relationships or form new ones within a local chapter of an organization you're targeting. The script below can be used with the head of a local organization or the person in charge of getting speakers.

―――

YOU: "Hi James. This is <introduce yourself>. I noticed that you have speakers once a month at your meetings. You've had some really interesting speakers in the past year!" *<Note: upfront research allows you to speak in their vernacular about the topics they're interested in.>*

PROSPECT: "Yes. Mr. Darwin gave a great presentation... <continues for a bit>. Are you interested in joining our group?"

YOU: "Actually, I might be able to do even better. I often speak to engineers about the upside of interplasmatic reference points. My most popular speech is 'The P-Spot: Your Production Line's Erogenous Zone.' Do you think your members would be interested in a presentation along those lines?" <*Obviously, you'll have to substitute your own killer title. Remember, it's about THEM, not you.*>

PROSPECT: "Whoa! That's funny. And a bit racy. Yeah, I bet that would draw a crowd. Let's talk about dates..."

Once you've knocked their socks off at a local meeting, it's fairly easy to obtain the name of the regional organizer and use your strong, local relationships, your killer title and the testimonial you'll obtain from the local chapter to get a regional gig. After a successful regional speech, your next step is the national stage.

4. *Tap your publisher's power*. If your book has recently been published, that will help immensely. Event organizers want the latest and greatest on their stage and, as the author of a newly published guide to success, you're the cat's meow. If your book is commercially published, prod the publisher's marketing group into action (not the easiest task). The more good books you publish, the easier it will be to win speaking gigs, and the higher the fee you'll be paid.

5. *Self host*. As I mentioned above, the easiest way to get a speaking gig is to hire yourself! Pulling in an audience is another matter, though. The keys to a successful, self-hosted event are: 1) a killer topic, 2) an anchor attendee, 3) partners.

We've already discussed a killer topic. The same rules that apply to developing a speech title apply to your self-hosted event. Even when your intent is to assemble a panel, facilitate an executive roundtable, or coordinate a conference, you'll need an alluring, central theme.

A TALE OF TWO SPEECHES

If your name isn't an instant draw, then find someone who is and do whatever it takes to get his commitment to attend. Then you can tell others, "Bill Gates will be there." Increase your odds of locking in a big name anchor attendee by organizing your self-hosted event around an existing conference. Find out the timing of a well-attended conference, then book a meeting room for the day before, one of the evenings, or the morning after. That approach also helps if your target is spread across the country (or world).

Partners extend your reach and increase your potential audience. By the way, competitors are often the best partners for events like this. (See the bonus resource, **Borrowing Audiences and Building Your Tribe**, which also is useful for your digital presence activities.)

General Session Speaker or Breakout Leader?

Given the choice between being on the main stage in front of 500 conference attendees versus leading one of five simultaneous breakout sessions for 100 people, always choose the breakout.

What? Doesn't the main stage at the Intergalactic Bakery Association conference grant you far more exposure and set you up as *the* authority? You bet it does. And you should definitely aim for the main stage *in addition* to a breakout, because when Yuri Yusimi from Sereus Dough, Inc. shows up at your breakout, you know he actively chose to hear you speak. Clearly, he believes the problem you solve is a higher priority than the ones being addressed by other breakout speakers.

Plus, it's easier to run an interactive session that creates a personal connection with a group of twenty or 100 than with a group of 200 or 1,000. Whenever I'm asked to speak on the main stage, I always request a breakout session as part of the package. Usually the conference organizer is surprised but pleased, and I walk away with more clients.

How to Give a Bang-Up, Better-than-Chocolate Speech

You can count the keys to delivering an outstanding, client-winning speech on one hand. Here's my five-finger approach in a nutshell:

1. *Open strong*. First impressions are critical and set the tone for the rest of the speech. Work on a hook, a story, a factoid, or some other way to instantly engage your audience.

2. *Focus*. Make three points in nine ways rather than twenty-seven different points. No audience remembers more than three lessons anyway. More is not better. More is confusing and diluting.

3. *Interact*. Talking heads can be interesting, but an interactive discussion draws prospects in and connects them with you. While it's a bit more challenging, you can run a dynamic, engrossing and highly interactive session with hundreds of participants if you know the right techniques.

4. *Regale*. Stories and metaphors are required. Make your message easy to visualize, easy to grasp, and concrete. A story can accomplish all three.

5. *Close and collect*. The emotion your audience is feeling when you walk off the stage is the emotion they'll associate with you. If your energy peters out, so will their interest in working with you. Therefore, close strong, and have some mechanism in place to collect contact information.

Follow-Up After Your Speech

Connecting with prospects soon after your speech is like having the guy at the corner mini-mart give you a few thousand free Powerball tickets. It increases your odds of seeing a major cash influx by a few orders of magnitude. But if you're like most consultants, you may not be sure exactly how to follow up or what to say to Yuri Yusimi and the other attendees. We're going to solve that right now.

If your speech was attended by fewer than fifty people, you're going to call *every single attendee*, two-to-three days after the speech. It's easy to make twenty-five calls in a day if you have their contact information. (If you're not sure of the best way to obtain contact information, download this bonus resource: **Four Killer Approaches for Collecting Contact Information at a Speech**.)

Whether you get them in person or have to leave a voicemail, you're going to say the exact same thing:

～vvvv～

YOU: "Hi, Yuri, this is <introduce yourself>. You attended my P-spot presentation on Monday. I like to follow up with everyone who's attended one of my sessions because I know that sometimes questions come up a day or two later. So I wanted to make myself available in case you had questions. And, of course, to get any feedback."

～vvvv～

If your speech was attended by more than fifty people, follow the "Communication Gap" method I detail in a downloadable bonus called **The Fast, Easy & Effective Follow-Up Approach for Speeches to Large Audiences**. It's highly effective and an efficient method to land multiple new clients.

We've talked about where to write and where to speak and you may have noticed a common theme: trade associations are an outstanding venue for your marketing. In fact, trade associations can be so instrumental to your success that they deserve some love and attention all on their own. Let's give them their chocolate valentine next.

BONUS MATERIAL

Bonus Materials available at davidafields.com/winningclients

Borrowing Audiences and Building Your Tribe

Four Killer Approaches for Collecting
Contact Information at a Speech

The Fast, Easy & Effective Follow-Up
Approach for Speeches to Large Audiences

CHAPTER 11

Trade Associations

Trade Association participation may seem like a minor league marketing vehicle compared to the other four Marketing Musts. However, this marketing approach can be the Stanley Cup of business development. (If you're not a hockey nut like me, you can settle for the Super Bowl of business development. World Series? Preakness?)

I've seen more consultants generate clients through active, trade association participation than any other marketing approach. Plus, focusing on trade associations is easy to do and complements your efforts in writing, speaking, networking, and increasing your digital presence.

Take the case of Tori, an HR specialist in Toronto, whose large network of contacts had generated a steady stream of clients when she first jumped into independent consulting. Then came a two-year hiatus while she cared for her ailing parents. Sadly, while attending to her parents, her contact list and resume grew painfully cold, and when I met her, Tori had already spent a fruitless year struggling to resuscitate her consulting business.

Her fortunes changed as soon as she joined the local chapter of a large trade association. Tori immediately jumped onto an important committee and volunteered to lead a project on a *pro bono* basis. Within two months, one of the other participants on her committee had hired her for a lucrative gig, and the trade association itself hired her to perform follow-on work. That was the jumpstart Tori needed to get her practice back on track.

The Four Keys to Marketing via Trade Associations

1. *Focus.* Fortunately, trade associations are inherently focused. The best, most active trade associations that are ripe with opportunities are fairly specialized. They serve a particular function, or industry, or both. Joining one or two trade associations will encourage you to focus your firm and, by doing so, increase your impact.

2. *Active Participation.* Simply putting your name on a list or attending a conference won't generate clients, or even speaking gigs or writing opportunities. Join a committee or two. Take on a project for them the way Tori did. Participate on advisory boards. Sit down with the executive directors and get to know their needs. Right-Side Up thinking is paramount here; your primary concern should be what the trade association needs, not what it can do for you.

3. *Consistency/Longevity.* The value of attending conferences and trade shows used to escape me. Then I discovered the importance of consistency and longevity. Plan on at least a three-year commitment, and here's why:

   The first time you attend the Intergalactic Bakery Association's annual conference you'll meet many prospects, encounter more than a few other consultants, and wonder in the subsequent months why you didn't land any clients. The next year you'll see some of the same people and be familiar to them. The *third* year you engage the same people in conversation you'll be considered a friend, someone they trust and will turn to for business.

The same rule applies for participation on committees and for writing. Tons of consultants are flashes in the pan. They come and go from trade associations with a single article or after a few meetings with one committee. When you stick with it for a few years, you'll find your rewards suddenly multiply.

4. *Don't Pitch*. You'll get nowhere if you're perceived as a sales-person in search of business, rather than a member committed to helping. But then again, you already know that—it's Right-Side Up thinking.

How to Leverage a Trade Association

Trade associations are like a 7-Eleven convenience store for the other four Marketing Musts (without the Twinkies®). Creating a relationship with the executive director of the association unlocks the doors, and once you're inside, the other marketing tools are sitting on the shelf, easy pickings.

- *Writing*. Every trade association has some sort of publication. Most have multiple vehicles, including online newsletters and blogs and often a monthly or quarterly magazine. You can pen an article, host a column, or create a special publication. One very successful writing tactic is to lead a survey and create the report that goes out to members. That's high value to the association, grants terrific visibility, and positions you as a thought leader.

- *Speaking*. Of course, there are the regional and national meetings where you can take the stage. Don't forget about special interest subgroups inside the association. Those are the equivalent of breakout sessions: participants are more engaged and have more urgent needs.

  In addition, you could run a webinar for the association, lead a training session (paid or free), or facilitate roundtable meetings. All are opportunities to show off your smarts in front of dozens or hundreds of prospects.

- *Networking*. In addition to circulating at conferences, you can join committees, enlist in roundtable discussions, and participate in advisory groups. Leading or contributing to a project the way Tori did is also an excellent opportunity to build relationships with prospects.

- *Digital Presence*. Trade associations are relying more and more on digital means to reach their members. That's good news for you. Write for their blog and regularly add your comments to other's blog posts on the trade association's website, or grab a monthly column in their digital newsletter. You might consider conducting webinars or contributing to their twitter feed. Those are just a few of the possibilities for creating a digital presence.

Since we're on the topic of creating a digital presence, and that marketing strategy has quickly developed the all-star power of Wayne Gretzky[†] and the reach and influence of Shaquille O'Neal,[‡] let's take a closer look at digital presence now.

[†] The greatest hockey player of all time.

[‡] The hall-of-fame, LA Lakers star towers 7'1" tall, and has enormous reach in many ways.

CHAPTER 12

Digital Presence

One summer, over thirty years ago, I made good money as an interviewer for a dating service. (Best. Job. Ever.) If I tried replicating that summer job today I wouldn't make a dime because dating services now are 99 percent online. The consulting landscape has shifted almost as dramatically, though it's taken much longer.

IT'S "CLUNKER"... I SWIPE LEFT OR RIGHT TO FIND BRILLIANT-LOOKING CONSULTANTS

Only five years ago, I would have told you not to spend more than a few minutes worrying about your digital presence. Consulting is, after all, a personal, relationship-driven business and Sereus Dough, Inc. will hire you because Yuri Yusimi knows you, not because they found you on the business equivalent of a dating site.

Boy, have times changed. Dialing up your digital presence is an absolute must in your plan to build a bigger or more profitable consulting practice.

A couple of quick caveats: as with each of the Five Marketing Musts, there are books and courses galore that detail every nuance and detail of digital presence. This chapter will give you an overview *from a consulting point of view.* Further, what's correct at the time of this writing may be out of date one year from now. Take these recommendations as a *starting point* for your digital presence efforts.

The Five Most Important Digital Presence Tactics for Consultants

Your digital presence should revolve around five tactics:

- Website
- Periodic Content
- One-Off Content
- Webinars
- Social Media

Let's dig into each one a bit more.

Website

Operating any business without a website these days is foolhardy. The very first place a prospect turns to after they hear your name is your website. Therefore, it's worth keeping your website up-to-date and as resource-rich as possible in order to create a good impression.

There are two different types of websites: those meant to generate an immediate sale and those meant to facilitate a long-term sale. As consultants, we're interested in the long-term, super-high ticket sale.

TWO TYPES OF WEBSITES

IMMEDIATE SALE
> VISIT PRODUCES A SALE
> ANSWERS QUESTIONS
> DETAILS VALUE
> E-COMMERCE FOCUSED

LONG-TERM SALE
> VISIT PRODUCES CONTACT INFO
> PROMOTES QUESTIONS
> TEASES VALUE
> CONTACT FOCUSED

Website designers tend to concentrate on aesthetics and the latest, coolest technology. They build pretty sites that visitors wander around randomly before darting off to another site. That's a waste. Guide your visitors through a relationship-building interaction by focusing on what you want them to *Do, Think,* and *Feel* at every point on your site.

In fact, I recommend you make a detailed Do/Think/Feel list for every page on your site and insist that your website designer treat the list as the primary objective. Aesthetics should take a back seat— they're important, but not driving the bus. For example, you might come up with the following list for your home page:

Table 12-1

I WANT A VISITOR TO MY HOME PAGE TO...		
DO (Priority Order)	**THINK**	**FEEL**
1. Call me 2. Download my ebook 3. View my services	• I'm an expert in chocolate tasting • I solve an urgent problem they have • They want to know more	• Intrigued • Connected with me

Based on that input, your home page design may place your phone number very prominently on the page, and include a promotion for your ebook "above the fold." The menu bar may start with *Services* or highlight that choice in some way. The page would feature a picture of you smiling while tasting a wide array of chocolates. Perhaps there's a subhead asking, "Want to know more...?" with a link to a contact page with, again, your phone number in a large font.

That's just an example, of course, and it's only one page of the site. To help, I've posted a simple, **Do/Think/Feel Template for Designing Your Website** as a bonus resource.

Remember Right-Side Up thinking, though:

Your website may offer a bit of information about you, but the focus of the site shouldn't really be about you... it should be about your prospects!

Show you understand your prospects' situation, their problems, and their aspirations. Speak to what they will gain, not what you will do. Talk about the experience they will have if they engage you, not the process you go through. Include testimonials that demonstrate your familiarity with prospects' situations, while minimizing testimonials that just shout about your greatness.

The simple questions that will keep your website Right-Side Up are, "What do my prospects really want to know? What's important to them?"

Periodic Content

Blogs, podcasts, and emailed newsletters produce a steady, periodic flow of content. The minimum frequency is about once per quarter. You won't generate a large body of work quickly if you're only issuing your words of wisdom four times a year (unless you're producing a magazine each time). However, that low frequency is sufficient for keeping your name in clients' minds.

Some consultants post a blog, or publish a podcast online and expect their phones to ring immediately. They're missing the point. The whole idea behind your periodic, online content is to keep you top of mind and support your relationship (more on that in Step 4:

Connect, Connect, Connect). As long as Yusimi thinks of you when he starts searching for a solution, your ongoing, digital marketing has done its job. In the consumer products world, we used to call this reminder advertising.

One-Off Content

Sure, we think Einstein was pretty smart with the whole $E=mc^2$ thing, and his pithy aphorisms. But don't forget that his original paper on special relativity was 30 pages long. Yes, short and pithy content like blogs, newsletters, and podcasts is more important than ever, but those formats convey only a tiny slice of the smarts you have to offer your clients.

Einstein needed to build his reputation with in-depth vehicles and you do, too. In the digital world, your one-off vehicles can include articles, white papers, detailed infographics, videos, and ebooks. Over the long term, you'll create a presence as a knowledgeable expert or a thought leader, and you'll generate more clients through your one-off content than periodic content.

Many consultants have one-off content on their to-do lists but never seem to get it *off* the list and into the world. If Einstein had never published his theory of relativity, we wouldn't have accurate GPS devices and I'd *still* be getting lost every day I venture out in a car.

Your ideas are valuable. But if you let your deep thinking about interplasmatic bakery nodes sit in the someday/maybe pile, Yuri Yusimi (and 1,000 other prospects) will never see it. Get help! Content creation is a huge industry now, and a bevy of ghostwriters, videographers, and all other ilk of content producers are within easy reach. Hire good freelancers to convert the myriad ideas in your head into valuable content you can post online.

Webinars

I'm calling out webinars specifically because they're the online equivalent of speaking. Remember that speaking gigs take a long time to secure, but they're uber powerful in terms of reputation building. Webinars deliver a high-impact reputation punch similar to an in-person speech but with a much shorter sales cycle. There's a good reason webinars have become a pervasive marketing vehicle. They should be a prominent part of your digital presence, too.

The hardest part about webinars is getting attendees. Partners are your answer. Join forces with magazines, associations, and even other consultants who can extend your reach among your target audience. (See the bonus resource, **Borrowing Audiences and Building Your Tribe.**)

Of course, you also need a relevant, compelling topic! Developing the right webinar title is half the battle, and you'll enjoy much higher success if you devote time to brainstorming, soliciting feedback and tweaking your title ideas.

Social Media

No matter what the gurus say, social media is still very much the Wild West. It's a high-promise, ever-changing landscape of opportunity where you can spend a fortune and end up with nothing but tumbleweeds.

At the moment, the only social media outlets worth focusing on by consultants are LinkedIn™ and Twitter™. That's bound to change as younger generations make their way into the upper tiers of management. But for now, you can probably restrict your attention to those two venues.

For consultants, Twitter's primary purpose is to drive prospects to your other digital presence vehicles, such as your website, blog, podcast or an upcoming webinar. The golden rule of twitter is to provide value first and promote *only* with value. Right-Side Up thinking prevails again.

LinkedIn is emerging as a viable path to obtaining clients, but it's not a totally reliable route. Best practices for consultants are few and far between. I've not yet met a consultant who's won a six-figure project directly from LinkedIn outreach; however, that could definitely happen in the not-too-distant future.

Based on the consultants I've worked with, only a handful of whom have secured business via LinkedIn, my two words of advice are, "careful planning." LinkedIn works best when you map out a deliberate communication path that moves a connection from new contact to relationship to client, offering value at each stage. With a deliberate, detailed approach in place, LinkedIn can be a highly useful first step in creating new connections. Without that well-planned system, LinkedIn is just an unproductive social club.

The Importance of Specificity and Relevance in Digital Presence

In the pre-Internet world, if you wanted to learn how to fix the leak under your sink, you might check out a few plumbing-related books from your library. Then you'd flip through hundreds of pages to find the two pages you need. Now you search online for "fixing a PVC trap under a sink" and ten relevant links pop up that will answer your question.

The digital world is massive and, at the same time, completely searchable. As a result, prospects expect to find exactly the content they need amidst an avalanche of information from thousands of sources. The only way to be effective in that environment is to be intensely focused and specific with your content.

Similarly, the key to converting a digital contact into a client is quickly establishing your reputation as a source of value. The secret to that is ensuring your content is relevant. Thanks to your hard work in Step 2: Maximize Impact, your online IP will be relevant, meaningful, attention-grabbing, and an enticing invitation to call you for help.

For instance, Don, the consultant I mentioned in Chapter 9 generates a steady flow of client inquiries through the content on his website. He focuses on helping small companies build compensation plans and his white papers rise to the top whenever a small company researches the topic online.

I've had a similar experience. When I first started Ascendant Consulting about 10 years ago I penned an in-depth white paper on a topic I knew well from my trade marketing experience. It bore the eminently sexy title, "Consumer Products SKU Rationalization." I knew nothing about search engine optimization (SEO) or digital presence when I wrote it, but I figured posting the sixteen-page piece couldn't hurt.

Ten years later, if you Google "SKU rationalization" my white paper still comes up on the first page. As a result, I receive a steady trickle of prospects who contact me out of the blue looking for help in that area, including an email on the very day I was writing this section of the book. Why does that old white paper generate business? The target is obvious and narrow (consumer products marketers) and the problem I'm solving is extremely specific (SKU rationalization).

Inbound and Outbound Exposure in the Digital World

The easiest way to think about gaining digital exposure is dividing it into *Inbound* and *Outbound* efforts. Inbound is when Diane Decisionmaker, whom you've never heard of, finds you online. She harbors the motive force. Outbound is when you're actively reaching out to Yuri Yusimi and other prospects you know through some online mechanism. You're the motive force.

Inbound digital presence includes your website, content that you post online, and links from other sites, as well as any SEO efforts. The goal is to be findable, to be the nugget of gold a prospect spots amidst a riverbed of rocks. And as I said earlier, while there are many nuances and an entire industry built around making you findable online, the drivers of success remain constant: specificity and relevance.

Bottom line: The best, next step you can take to improve your digital presence, no matter which online tactics you choose, is to tighten up your message.

OOH, LOOK. WE SHOULD HIRE
THAT BAKERY EXPERT

The Numbers Trap

Exposure is where digital presence really shines as a marketing vehicle. With a small amount of effort you can reach far more prospects through digital marketing than via any analog equivalent, and in a fraction of the time. But don't fall into the meaningless numbers trap.

It's easy to get swept up into a world where you're totally focused on generating more followers, more hits, and more connections. But rather than chanting "More, more, more," your mantra should be "Engaged and high potential."

You're better off with a circulation of twenty-five interested decision makers than with a list of 25,000 irrelevant recipients who instantly delete your emails. This applies to every aspect of digital presence, where the bulk of marketers are still focused on buying a large crowd rather than a highly engaged club.

What's next? You've met four of the Five Marketing Musts, and now it's time to take a deep breath and spend time with the patriarch of the family: networking. Networking is such a critical and pervasive part of a consultant's marketing efforts that it deserves it's very own Step in the business development process. No consulting business can thrive without relationships, and no new relationships can be developed unless we know how to connect with people.

Ready to start exploring the all-important nuances of building and nurturing effective, long lasting relationships? I thought so. Let's jump into Step 4: Connect, Connect, Connect.

BONUS MATERIAL

Bonus Materials available at davidafields.com/winningclients

Do/Think/Feel Template for Designing Your Website

Borrowing Audiences and Building Your Tribe

Connect, Connect, Connect

(Create Relationships and Opportunities)

Every winter, tens of thousands of people stare at a dark, pine tree while millions observe it on TV. A switch is flipped and, in an instant, 45,000 colored lights blaze and glitter amidst Swarovski crystals.

People cheer, point, laugh and kiss. All sparked by some electrical connections at Rockefeller Center.

Connections are the key. We're in a deeply human profession. All the flashy content may be in place, but it's personal connections that spark emotions, prompt action and result in project opportunities.

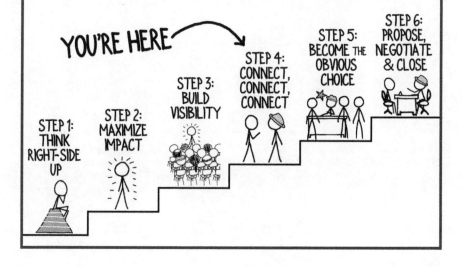

YOU'RE HERE

STEP 1: THINK RIGHT-SIDE UP

STEP 2: MAXIMIZE IMPACT

STEP 3: BUILD VISIBILITY

STEP 4: CONNECT, CONNECT, CONNECT

STEP 5: BECOME THE OBVIOUS CHOICE

STEP 6: PROPOSE, NEGOTIATE & CLOSE

CHAPTER 13

Creating Relationships

The next four chapters could be thought of as "meaty," but that would be highly awkward for an author who's a longtime vegetarian. Instead, let's call them "rich"—rich in content and, when you complete this step, you'll be wealthy. You see? It fits together like a warm, chocolate brownie and vanilla ice cream.

Some people define wealth as the amount of money they have, or material goods they possess, or the freedom to use their time as they please. Not me. I define wealth as relationship strength. To me, relationships are *everything*.

**The more, strong, vibrant, enriching relationships
a person has, the wealthier he is.**

Medical research has shown that people who are surrounded by loved ones and good friends live healthier, longer lives. I know from almost 20 years of weekly volunteer work at an assisted living home that at the end of your life your bank account, fancy car, and free time don't hold a candle to your family and friends.

The fact is, you can win consulting business without marketing, without optimizing your impact, without knowing how to put together a compelling proposal, or without pricing your project well. But you can't win without relationships. No executive is going to hand you $2.5 million or $250,000 or even $25,000 without having some sort of one-on-one relationship with you. That's why I'll say it again: *relationships are everything.*

Relationships = Wealth

If you embrace my *relationships = wealth* philosophy, it will transform what you do and how you do it. For instance, you'll naturally embrace Right-Side Up thinking, endeavor to determine what others need, and build relationships in order to enable others' success. Ironically, this relationships-focused orientation will create better financial results than the typical, money-focused worldview.

Since relationships are the engine powering your consulting firm, we have a lot of ground to cover. That ground can be summarized as: Create, Nurture, and Leverage relationships. The next few pages focus on overall approaches and strategies for establishing relationships. Chapter 14 dives into nurturing relationships, then we'll continue the topic of nurturing by drilling down into the granular details of outreach in Chapter 15.

We round out the business of Connect, Connect, Connect by leveraging relationships in Chapter 16. Some people think consulting is about connecting the dots. You know better. It's about connecting the people!

The Master Strategy for Creating Relationships

Your most reliable and productive source of *new* relationships (and clients) should be introductions and referrals from *existing* clients.

That's already the case for many consultants, but if your current and past clients aren't regularly introducing you to new prospects, then maybe it's time to examine two parts of your business: 1) your project quality, and 2) your discipline in asking for referrals and introductions.

Your clients need to see that you do great work and produce concrete results. No matter what type of consulting you do, the outcomes can be made explicit and tangible for your clients.

For example, even if the output of your consulting engagement is an abstract recommendation, you can deliver it as a memorable infographic. If you're coaching an individual, your coachee's progress can be measured through surveys. Concrete benefits highlight your value to your clients, and that encourages them to introduce you to others.

Unfortunately, even if you're producing phenomenal work and making the results concrete, most of your clients will rarely spontaneously introduce you to other prospects. Why? Because they're thinking about their issues and priorities, not about you. So what do you do?

You have to ask your clients for introductions.

ASKING FOR INTRODUCTIONS MUST BECOME A ROUTINE PART OF YOUR CONSULTING WORK

How to Ask for Introductions

If this is starting to feel uncomfortable, don't worry. You're about to learn an easy, comfortable technique to use, called the "Transfer of Interest." First, look at the old-fashioned way of asking for introductions, which sounds something like this:

———

BOB: "Yuri, as you know I help bakery companies improve their operations. Who do you know that would benefit from the value I provide?"

———

Ugh. You've probably read something like that in sales books or heard it recommended by gurus. But I bet you almost never say it because it feels as pushy and graceless as a twelve-year-old trying to get a first date. It's also as painful for your client to hear as it is for you to say. The person you're asking has to wrack his brains, thinking about whether the people he knows actually have the problem you solve. Does he know that? No.

On top of that, he's worried that you're going to hard-sell his contact, and that will reflect badly on him. It adds up to one, big negative. If you've only known that traditional line, I understand why you wouldn't use it!

The Transfer of Interest
(A pain-free way to ask for an introduction)

The Transfer of Interest is far more effective and much, much easier to say. Here's an example of how this technique sounds with a current client:

―――

YOU: "Yuri, you've been incredibly helpful during this project. You know that meeting people and building relationships are at the heart of what I do. Plus, I love meeting interesting people. Who have you run into recently who's intriguing, creating change or shaking things up?"

―――

You're not asking for a sale. You're merely asking for an interesting connection. Better yet, you're asking Yusimi to recall someone he thinks is engaging or intriguing or making waves. That's much, much easier for him to deal with. He doesn't have to think about whether someone needs your services or not. Also, he doesn't worry about your tarnishing his relationship by hard-selling his contact.

You're asking him to consider his contacts in a favorable light. Not only does that wrap the introduction request in a positive frame, the interest he has in his colleagues subconsciously transfers to you. It's a win all around! Now you have a request that's easier to make and far easier for your contacts to answer.

Don't worry about the "quality" of the names you're given because the people you'll meet with this technique are more likely to be buyers. Interesting people—movers and shakers—are making things happen. They're hiring consultants. Besides, you never know who knows whom, and what connections will lead to new clients. Expanding your network is always good, and any new relationship boosts your personal affluence, even those that don't ultimately become substantive contributors to your business-development efforts.

When to Ask for Introductions

There's an easy rule to follow about when to ask for introductions: *all the time.* When you close a project, your new client is high on you, and it's a perfect time to ask for an introduction. When you lose a project, your prospective client is feeling bad about turning you down, and that's another great time to ask for introductions!

Mid-project, when you've had a success, ask for an introduction. (Don't forget to ask for a testimonial after a success, too.) Just before the project ends is another auspicious opportunity. You can even ask for introductions from people you've just met—your first conversation with a new contact can create an open window to ask for an introduction.

The First Conversation

Before we move on to other strategies for creating relationships, let's quickly cover what you say when you first reach out to a new contact. (By the way, you do this on the phone or in person, not email.) Ideally, your mutual contact introduced you, which makes your follow-up easy. But let's say all you received from Yuri was a name and contact information. Then you'll want to use a script like the following:

—*mm*—

YOU: "Hi, Sarah. My name is <your name>. I was chatting with Yuri Yusimi over at Sereus Dough and your name came up. Yuri said you're one of the savviest plant managers he's met, and thought we'd enjoy meeting each other. With a description like that, I couldn't resist reaching out to you. Do you have a few minutes to chat now or could we set a time to talk..."

—*mm*—

I've found that a bit of flattery (if it's sincere) goes a long way, as does an approach that is casual and expressly *not* selling anything.

If you practice the scripts I've recommended, you'll find that asking for introductions is actually fun, and you'll get to meet a wide range of interesting people. Many will never turn into clients or even refer you to clients. That's okay. You're still becoming a wealthier person. On the other hand, some of those introductions will lead to new business, and that makes the process all the sweeter.

Five More Strategies for Creating Relationships

1. *Walk the halls.* When you win a project with a new client, it's like they're handing you a key to the bakery case. Suddenly, countless delicacies are within easy reach. Literally. When you're sitting in your client's office, other decision makers who could hire you are sitting in offices right down the hall.

   If you're a gregarious, outgoing person, all you have to do is knock on a nearby door, pop your head in, and introduce yourself:

―⁓―

YOU: "Hi, I'm <your name>. I'm working with Yuri on your bakery operations. I noticed you were just a couple of doors down and thought I'd introduce myself."

―⁓―

You generally can't go wandering all over a client site without permission, and you don't want your client bailing you out of the security office. However, the occupants of immediately adjacent offices are often in functions related to your project, and introducing yourself rarely goes astray.

If that seems a bit too forward or uncomfortable for you, then ask your client to make some introductions. For instance, if Yuri Yusimi is the VP in charge of one product line, perhaps VPs on other product lines are nearby, or an EVP or the CEO. It's a pretty simple request:

―⁓―

YOU: "Yuri, on the way to lunch would you mind introducing me to your CEO? I'd love to meet her."

―⁓―

2. *Set up an internal meeting*. A similar approach to walking the halls, but a bit more shrewd and deliberate, is conducting in-person sessions at the client's location that allow you to meet more decision makers. On virtually every project I manage, regardless of the industry or issue, I build in an opportunity to interview a wide range of people inside the organization. The rationale is simple: additional perspective and other ways of considering the problem are always valuable.

In most projects, you can also schedule a kickoff meeting, a work session, or final presentation that is broadly attended— all are easy ways to meet decision makers across the client's organization.

3. *Set up an external meeting*. Another method for leveraging an existing engagement is setting up meetings with new contacts who could contribute valuable information related to the assignment. Customers, key opinion leaders, experts, and even competitors may pony up insights that are valuable for your client. Benchmarking the competition and collecting industry best practices can contribute to your client's success, *and* open the door to a ton of new relationships with high-potential prospects.

A word of caution: Do *not* sell or solicit these new prospects while you are collecting information for your client. It is inappropriate and will reflect badly on you.

4. *Set up interviews*. You can target prospects, key opinion leaders, and experts even if you're not working on a project. How? By researching an article, survey or some other piece of thought leadership. A media consultant in Toronto told me he writes a weekly article for his trade association's blog because it gives him an excuse to contact every prospect in the entire industry. He can ask for examples, opinions, responses to other people's opinions, and so forth. Let's say Yusimi gave you the name of an industry bigwig named Paulette Poundcake. A simple script for interviews sounds like this...

—ww—

> YOU: "Hi, Paulette. My name is <your name>. I'm writing an article on plasmatic bakery nodes for *Baked Goods Today* and Yuri Yusimi over at Sereus Dough said I absolutely had to talk with you, that you're a truly innovative thinker in this arena. Do you have a couple of minutes?"

—ww—

Virtually everyone loves to be cast as an expert. Saying you want to highlight her in an article strokes her ego and starts the relationship off on a positive note. Of course, at the end of the interview, you ask Paulette for introductions. That makes the next rounds of interviews easier to secure.

5. *Make it interactive.* All the visibility-building approaches outlined in Step 3: Build Visibility put you in a great position to meet new prospects – *if you make them interactive.* For instance, all your writing can (and should) include a request for comments and input from readers.

Similarly, if you're giving a speech, you have the opportunity to interview key individuals to help you tailor your material. During the speech you can conduct interactive exercises that instantly connect you to members of the audience. For instance, when I'm speaking to large audiences, I often ask listeners to write down their response to a question, then I ask members of the audience to stand up when I describe the response that matches what they wrote.

Of course, after your speech, don't run off before you have a chance to meet the many people who want to get to know you.

The five strategies I just outlined, plus the Transfer of Interest are a good start for rapidly building your network.

Follow-Up

Any successful salesperson will tell you the one thing that separates rainmakers from order-takers is follow-up. After you meet new people, no matter what the vehicle or venue, you *must* follow up with them.

The subject of the follow-up conversation is determined by the content of your first conversation. If they explicitly said they wanted to learn more about your offerings, then that's a fair topic to broach. But in most cases, your follow-up call will be Right-Side Up: all about them and their world.

To be clear, establishing a relationship and thinking Right-Side Up does not necessarily mean talking about the kids and hockey. (Although most conversations are better if hockey is involved.) Establishing a relationship means listening and talking without pitching business. Here's how a follow-up conversation could start:

~~~

YOU: "Hi Yuri, this is (your name). We met at the bakery conference last week. During the late afternoon break we chatted and you mentioned a number of ideas you had about node placement. What you said really stuck with me and I'd love to hear more about your thoughts and what you're doing over at Sereus Dough. Is this a good time to chat for a few minutes?"

~~~

If the person you're talking to abhors small talk and wants to jump into brass tacks, then get down to business—their business, not yours. Let the prospect drive the shift from non-business to business topics. You'll sense when they're ready to change gears, and then you can use "The Turn," which is a carefully scripted segue that I'll introduce in Chapter 16.

Dos and Don'ts of Creating Relationships

No matter how strongly you believe in establishing new relationships, the practical execution may still feel fraught with danger and unknowns. The following Dos and Don'ts list will provide a handy guide to keep you headed in the right direction.

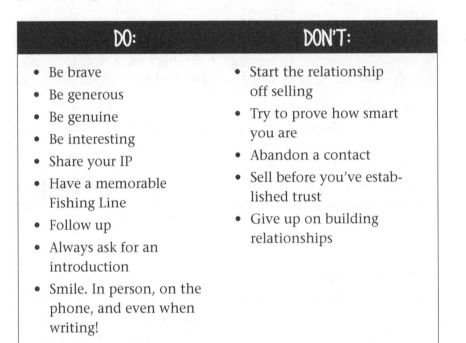

DO:	DON'T:
• Be brave	• Start the relationship off selling
• Be generous	• Try to prove how smart you are
• Be genuine	• Abandon a contact
• Be interesting	• Sell before you've established trust
• Share your IP	• Give up on building relationships
• Have a memorable Fishing Line	
• Follow up	
• Always ask for an introduction	
• Smile. In person, on the phone, and even when writing!	

If the act of meeting someone instantly created a vibrant, rich relationship, then everyone would be wealthy. After all, we each meet hundreds or thousands of people over the span of our lives. But each new contact is only a seed. That seed must be nurtured to become a strong, healthy addition to your garden. Nurturing relationships is an art—an art that you're going to master next.

CHAPTER 14

Nurturing Relationships

Knowing a person and building a relationship with him are two entirely differ-ent kettles of fish. It's the difference between the planks of wood in my garage and the dining room table I still haven't built; between a block of marble and the statue of David. The former is merely potential and the latter is truly valuable.

Michelangelo purportedly remarked that he simply chipped away the parts of the block that weren't David. You now have a ware-house full of connections—they're your blocks of marble. When you transform those connections into relationships, the potential for wealth and business success is unleashed.

I HAVE RELEASED YOU FROM THE STONE

UH, THANKS. I STILL FEEL A BIT STUCK.

How, exactly, do you cultivate rich relationships?

Earlier in my career, I thought that once you established a connection with a prospect, you were supposed to overwhelm him with so much value that he couldn't help but work with you. Under that rubric, each time you reach out to Yuri Yusimi at Sereus Dough, Inc. you're expected to send a relevant article or make a useful introduction or provide blazingly insightful feedback.

The assumption is that if you continuously add value, Yusimi will look at you favorably and bestow consulting projects. That's what many consultants are taught. That's how you win business, right?

Actually, no. There are two big problems with that thinking:

1. *It adds pressure*. The need to add value puts too much pressure on you and the relationship. When I look through consultants' contact lists and ask why they haven't reached out to this VP of Marketing or that General Manager, they invariably say something like, "I'm not sure what to say. I don't know how I would add value." If you feel as though you have to add value every time you reach out, it's no wonder your outreach efforts are stymied.

2. *It's self-serving*. Your need to add value is actually self-serving, especially if, in your heart, you're hoping to benefit from the "law of reciprocity," which suggests that if you provide value to Yusimi, he'll feel compelled to provide value back to you. Sorry, self-serving activities aren't the path to winning new consulting business. They're also as transparent as a teenager finally cleaning his room just before he happens to want to borrow the car.

When you enter each conversation with Yusimi thinking, "How can I win business from this person?" your motive is obvious to him, no matter how smooth your conversational skills are. And even when you pile on value, if it's clear you're in sales mode, Yusimi will resist your advances.

The fact is, you *don't* have to constantly add value to strengthen your personal bond. There's a world of difference between reaching out to a contact to try to find business, versus connecting with him to nurture the relationship while being *alert for opportunities*. And trust me, your contacts will feel it.

THE POINT OF NURTURING RELATIONSHIPS ISN'T TO SELL BUSINESS; IT'S TO MAKE THOSE RELATIONSHIPS STRONGER.

As I stated in the last chapter, I believe personal wealth is defined by your relationships—the more, strong relationships you have, the wealthier you are. So, to me, the purpose of nurturing relationships is self-evident: *it makes you wealthier*. But even if you don't agree with my definition of wealth, nurturing relationships is critical to your consulting business.

Relationships are the lifeblood of your practice, and the health of your practice is a direct reflection of the strength of the relationships you have with the Right People. (Remember them from Chapter 4?) Strong relationships create space for business opportunities to appear, and when opportunities do pop up, a strong relationship will support your winning a project.

Should You Be Nurturing or Discovering?

When you're talking with a prospect and the conversation shifts to how you could help him address a *specific* problem or aspiration, you move into discovery mode. That shift happens either because your prospect asks whether you can help or because you use "The Turn," as described in Chapter 16.

Once that shift happens you're in a discussion about doing business together, and you should jump right to Step 5: Become the Obvious Choice.

For instance, let's say Yuri Yusimi, our favorite plant manager calls you out of the blue to ask whether you can optimize his interplasmatic nodes. Bingo, you're in pursuit of a specific project! Jump to Step 5 and give your friends a high-five along the way.

WHEN TO MOVE FROM STEP 4 TO STEP 5

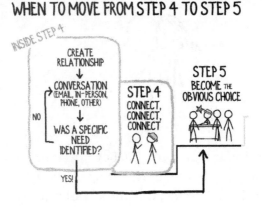

At all other times (i.e., the vast majority of the time), your conversations should nurture relationships and strengthen your bonds with your contacts. You're building a low-pressure, high-trust connection, and creating space for folks like Yusimi to turn to you when they're in need.

The Reality of Nurturing Relationships

By using all or most of the strategies you discovered in the previous chapter, you've now established relationships with a long list of new contacts. Bam, instant overwhelm! There's no feasible way to take 50 people out to lunch every week for one-on-one discussions, not to mention 500 or 5,000 contacts as you continue to grow your network.

How can you nurture relationships effectively and efficiently? Which relationships are most important, how often should you do something, and what, exactly, is needed? I'm so glad you asked!

Let's tackle the first couple of questions now, and in Chapter 15 we'll delve into the nitty-gritty details of building relationships via outreach efforts.

Who You Should Nurture: Targeting Your Network Core

We're going to divide your contact list in two. One crowd—your network core—is going to receive much more love from you than the other, larger, crowd. To find your network core, you're going to assign every person on your contact list a letter and a number.

IT'S LIKE PLACING COLORED STICKY NOTES ON EACH PERSON'S FOREHEAD THEN SAYING, "EVERYONE WITH A GREEN STICKY STAND UP. I'M TAKING YOU OUT TO LUNCH TODAY." ... SORT OF.

Segment Your Prospects by Relationship Strength

The letter you'll assign each person is either A, B or C. An A is for people with whom you have a strong relationship, strong enough that they'd call you back if you called them or shoot you a reply if you sent them an email. If you're married, your spouse should be an A, even if one of you is from Mars and the other from Venus. Your employees, subcontractors, and most clients should be As, even if some of them seem like they're from another planet too.

Assign a B to people with whom you have a decent relationship, but not strong enough to categorize them as an A. Maybe you've met with them once or twice but haven't touched base in a couple of years. Finally, assign a C to everyone else. These are people whose contact information you have for one reason or another but you don't really have any relationship to speak of.

Then Segment Your Prospects by Influence

Now go back through your list and assign everyone a 1, 2 or 3. Label people who can hire you directly with a 1. Think of a 1 as a decision maker. CEOs, division presidents, general managers, and maybe even vice presidents can be decision makers. The intern probably isn't.

Assign a 2 to anyone who can influence the decision to hire you but doesn't have the authority or position to bring you in. Sometimes these are technical experts. Other times they are just highly influential people—key opinion leaders, thought leaders, and well-respected figures within your industry.

Everyone else warrants a 3. Nice people to know, but they don't have much impact on your ability to win a project. The intern is assigned a 3, as is the Junior Assistant Deputy Desk Manager and the nice lady at the deli counter who seems to adore you, but the biggest win you'll receive from her is a free slice of cheese.

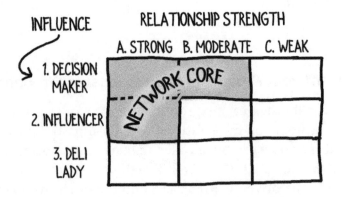

Now Identify Your Network Core

Your *network core*—the small crowd that's going to receive high levels of love and nurturing from you—are your A1s, B1s, and A2s. A1s are decision makers with whom you have a strong relationship. Your current clients are probably sporting that combination, and you definitely want to make your relationship with them your top priority! The B1s are prime candidates for relationship-building. The A2s in your network can introduce you to decision makers.

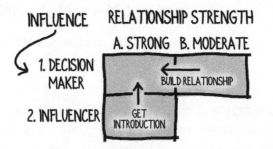

Over time you want to continuously monitor and build your network core. Can you imagine how strong your business would be if you had 150 A1s on your list? An extremely fertile pool of decision makers with whom you have a strong relationship would be a seven-figure network core.

If this segmentation exercise seems like considerable work, you're right. It's worth every minute of effort. Not only will your marketing efforts become more efficient, I guarantee you will uncover several, high-potential prospects who have been treading water, unnoticed in your sea of contacts.

All the tactics I'm about to outline are for you apply to your network core. Before we get there, though, what do you do with everyone else on your list?

Your Network Periphery

Everyone on your contact list who isn't in the core is in the periphery. That doesn't mean they're worthless or you shouldn't interact with them. You'll just nurture the relationship differently. Include your network periphery in all your mass outreach efforts.

Send them newsletters, for instance, and perhaps an annual or semi-annual email. In the old days this was called a "Christmas card list." Maybe it still is. If someone from the "low-love crowd" reaches out to you, terrific! Nothing says you can't do business with a contact on the periphery.

How Often to Contact Your Network Core

Touch every person in your network core regularly using one-to-one outreach *in addition to* any mass outreach efforts (i.e., your newsletter, podcasts, etc.).

Email: Send a personal email to everyone in your network core a minimum of one time per quarter. If a contact doesn't reply, wait at least a week to send another email, or just set them aside for another three months.

Phone: Reach out by phone directly to your network core a minimum of twice per year. If you reach out and the person doesn't call you back, give him at least a month before trying again.

In Person: Conduct in-person meetings only opportunistically, because in-person meetings are incredibly expensive in terms of time. Grabbing breakfast or dinner with a contact while you're visiting a city can be very effective. Or, if you can meet with a handful of contacts at one time, that could be worthwhile.

ANNUAL, PERSONAL OUTREACH

I've gone over a decade without meeting core contacts in person, and still won business from them. In person is great if it's convenient, and it unquestionably builds rich, personal bonds, but it doesn't need to be a set part of your relationship-building plan.

No matter what medium you use for your one-on-one outreach, do *not* mention previous attempts to reach someone. For instance, "I've called you six times and I would really love to chat with you." All that can do is make someone feel bad. There's no upside in terms of relationship building.

The exception to that rule is when you were expecting to hear from someone and they've totally disappeared. Then you can leave a message like, "I've called a few times and haven't heard from you, so I'm just checking to make sure you're okay." If you're going to leave a checking-in message like that, you have to be totally sincere and have a close enough relationship with your contact that it makes sense for you to be worried.

There are definitely best practices for each type of outreach, and Chapter 15 details exactly how to use outreach to build relationships, including phone scripts, voicemail scripts and more.

The Key Ingredients for Nurturing Relationships: Water, Sunshine, and Food

When you visualize someone you know, thoughts and feelings instantly bubble up. When your contacts think of you, what's their immediate reaction? Do they picture you as a sweet peach or a rotten tomato? Actually, that's an apt analogy since healthy business relationships are like fruit-bearing plants: they require water, sunshine and a bit of nourishing food.

Water = Right-Side Up Thinking

Water is the most fundamental building block of all life on earth, including your relationships. *The water for your relationships is Right-Side Up thinking.* The more a person senses that you are sincerely attentive to him, the more warmly he views you. That's true in marriages, it's true in parenting, and it's true with business connections, too.

As a reminder, Right-Side Up thinking means you focus on your prospects' needs and aspirations; on *their* goals, challenges, and issues; on *their* interests and preoccupations. It doesn't mean they become the center of your world; rather it means you join them at the center of their world.

For instance, pay attention to how each of your contacts prefers to communicate. Does he favor email or the phone? A lengthy warm-up period before getting down to business, or a quick hello then jump to brass tacks? I have a client on the West Coast whose emails are always just a line or two. I also learned that he only reads the first couple of sentences in any email. No matter how important or extensive the subject, he just doesn't get past the second sentence. As you can imagine, my notes to him are brief and to the point.

Sunshine = Likability

Likability is our business sunshine: it warms up any relationship. Clients often claim they choose their consultants based on capability, not how much they like one advisor over another. In the same vein, some consultants flippantly suggest, "A client doesn't have to like you to work with you!"

Hogwash.

Dave, an L.A.-based consultant, had a project with a couple of pieces outside his skill set. He referred his client to me and to another consultant who is brilliant, but frequently acerbic. I won my piece; the other consultant walked away empty handed because the client saw no need to deal with his style.

There are a zillion consultants out there who are plenty smart, savvy, and experienced. No client feels compelled to work with a discourteous or arrogant person when an equally talented and far more likable consultant is available.

Strive to be the type of person you would want to work with while letting the best parts of your personality shine through in your marketing, emails, and conversations. Clients enjoy magnetic characters.

Similarly, your marketing materials should always include a smiling, relaxed image of you. Prospects will scan through your website, looking for a picture of you. They want to see whether you look friendly and seem like someone they would want to work with.

Call it superficial if you want, but it's human nature. The high school rules and rewards of popularity still operate to a certain extent in the business world. It pays to be the light-hearted soul everyone wants to be around, rather than emulate Grumpy—who was cute as a dwarf in *Snow White*, but not an ideal model for attracting clients.

If you're naturally quiet, shy, or grouchy, adopting this persona might feel daunting. Let me tell you a story. Growing up, I was more like Grumpy. Only a small percentage of my peers would have described me as likable. I worked hard at being more likable and creating more positive energy, and I've (mostly) succeeded. It's easier if you believe other people are interesting (which I genuinely do).

So trust me when I say it's possible to increase your emotional attractiveness because I've been there, done that. If a quant geek like me can do it, so can you. (In case of emergency, resort to Right-Side Up thinking and make your interactions about *them*.)

Food = Value

Finally, we get to the *value* piece of the relationship puzzle. But keep in mind, everything starts with Right-Side Up thinking and Likability. As long as you have those pieces in place, value plays an important role. *After* you've delivered water and sunshine, you can add a bit of relationship food. Below are eight quick and easy ways to make your interactions more explicitly useful for your contacts:

1. ***Send an article*** that's relevant or even just interesting. It doesn't have to be penned by you. Highlight a sentence or two that you think are particularly worth reading.

2. ***Send a book*** that's fun, inspiring or intriguing. Or all three. If you include your notes and key takeaways from the book, your contact will love you.

3. ***Send an app*** or a software recommendation that will make your contact's life easier.

4. ***Push back*** on his assertions, and tactfully redirect his thinking. Too few people in a top executive's life are willing to disagree thoughtfully.

5. ***Frame his problem*** so that his fuzzy issues become clear, or his seemingly intractable issue becomes eminently solvable.

6. ***Make an introduction*** to a contact that could support him, utilize his skills or help him grow.

7. ***Act as a sounding board***. Everyone needs a safe place to suggest half-baked ideas. If you're that safe space, you'll be a favorite, go-to resource.

8. ***Speak with candor***, honesty, and consideration. Most executives, regardless of level, are surrounded by people who tell white lies, appease them, or nod politely while ignoring them. Your attention and candid feedback won't go unnoticed.

As I said earlier, you can build a strong bond with a contact that leads to business without explicitly adding value during every connection. Simply reaching out injects positive energy into relationships and keeps them vibrant.

Think about your closest friends. Do you have to bring a bottle of wine every time you visit? Do you feel compelled to offer advice during every single phone call? Of course not. I bet that if you haven't heard from a close friend in a long time, you send a quick text message like, "I'm just checking in. How's everything going?" You feel better and you know they'll feel better when they receive your message.

That's all it takes in business, too. Check in. Touch base. Let your contacts know you care.

At first, some of the people you're reaching out to may wonder why you're calling if you're not selling anything. Some may even say they only want you to call when you have something to offer—the "I'm busy, why are you calling?" variety of executive. Even those folks actually appreciate a fifteen-second, "I was thinking about you," touch by email and phone. Over time it adds up in their mind to, "David cares about me. He's not always selling. Hmm, maybe I should ask him about this problem I'm having..."

Still, you may be wondering exactly what to write in an email or what to say in a phone call. Fair enough. Let's continue nurturing relationships by diving into the nitty-gritty of outreach.

CHAPTER 15

The Nitty-Gritty of Outreach

If ever there's a time for us to walk around in the weeds of business develop-ment, it's now, while we're discussing relationships. Down here in the dirty details is where many consultants struggle. I hear questions virtually every day from very smart, experienced practitioners: "What, precisely, should I write in an email?" "What should I say when I call someone?" "How much chocolate should I send you, David?"

Okay, I may not hear that last one too often. Nevertheless, the details of nurturing relationships are worth walking through. Let's delve into each of the major modes of communicating with your contacts:

- Email
- Phone
- In Person

Effectively Nurturing Relationships via Email

Broadcast emails, such as a regular newsletter, are a great tool for sustaining and feeding a relationship. Even if a contact doesn't open or read every one, the email keeps your name in the forefront of his mind.

Keep your broadcast emails simple. A format with multiple sections and articles doesn't necessarily add value, but it does necessarily add more work for you. One, hard-hitting paragraph will have far more impact than five, dull articles. Similarly, you don't need to include fancy graphics or images in your emails.

Though I'm a strong advocate for picking up the phone, there are definitely times when a simple email makes sense—for instance, if you find yourself idle for a few minutes but don't have enough time for a phone call, or if your contact responds to emails but not to phone calls. Also, emails are particularly good for sending high-value content, such as a new article you published or a link to a site you think your contact would enjoy.

A personal email to a contact can reference something from a previous conversation or simply be a one liner inviting him to engage in conversation. I've had success with emails like the following:

Hi, Yuri. We haven't talked in ages. Grab fifteen minutes on my schedule, and let's connect: myconsultingfirm.com/mycalendar.

The brevity of that email presages a brief, beneficial conversation—the type even busy executives appreciate. I give them a very clear directive (not request) without any fluff or confusing messages. And I have found that including a link to an online scheduling tool makes a huge difference. *Huge.*

Effectively Nurturing Relationships on the Phone

Phone calls are ideal for building relationships. While they're not as rich as in-person meetings, they take a fraction of the time; and if your contacts are far-flung, in-person meetings just aren't feasible. On the flip side, a phone call is 1,000 times richer than email.

Figure 15-1

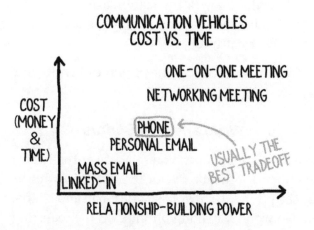

Despite the value of telephone conversations, many consultants dread picking up the phone to make outreach calls. I don't love making phone calls either, but I do them religiously because there is absolutely no denying the link between phone calls and revenue. That link holds for every consultant I've ever worked with.

Usually, the first call is the hardest to make. However, once you dial that first prospect, the next handful are much easier. Most consultants run out of steam by the tenth or fifteenth call, which is plenty!

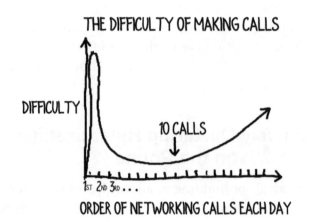

Figure 15-1

THE DIFFICULTY OF MAKING CALLS

DIFFICULTY

10 CALLS

1ST 2ND 3RD . . .

ORDER OF NETWORKING CALLS EACH DAY

If you think making phone calls is just for salespeople or it's an intrusion, flip back a couple of chapters and remind yourself that building relationships is a wealth-creation exercise. Not just for you; when you reach out, you're giving another person a chance to connect and build his wealth too!

Below are a few tips to make your phone call regimen easier and more effective:

Write and Use Scripts

If you're like most consultants, you rehearse virtually every conversation a few times (or maybe five or ten times) in your head before you pick up the phone. Then you get voicemail and all that rehearsal was wasted! No wonder making phone calls is exhausting.

On the other hand, if you have pre-written language that you use consistently, then you need much less energy each time you pick up the phone. You may find yourself rehearsing once or twice in your head for the first couple of calls, but by the third call you won't rehearse at all.

That's why I literally outline the entire flow of my standard outreach calls. Sure, I'll adjust what I say to reflect the actual conversation; however, the pre-work gets me started and that's usually the hardest part.

The outline I keep on my desk when I'm making outreach calls doesn't fit neatly into a book; however, you can download **David's Outreach Call Outline.**

If you download my outline you'll notice that my conversation flow always tries to direct the focus back to the person on the other side of the line. I'm not going to be obnoxious about it—there's always give and take in a conversation. But Right-Side Up thinking is the name of the game. I'm interested in their needs, their situation, their aspirations and their struggles.

Every conversation ends with:
1) scheduling the next phone call, and
2) a request for introductions.

Those two practices alone probably boost business by 30% or more each year, yet many consultants forget to do them.

You may want to develop a few different scripts or conversation flows based on the type of conversation (new introduction, old friend, etc.) or type of contact (investment banker, commercial baker, etc.). Usually the toughest piece is the very first couple of sentences out of your mouth, and scripting those can be a big help.

Your Voicemail Message

If you don't get someone on the phone, which will be most of the time, leave a strong voicemail message. The traditional approach to voicemails (which I don't love) is to tease with value. It sounds something like this:

―*᚜᚜᚜*―

YOU: "Hi, Yuri, this is *<your name, company and phone number>*. We haven't talked in forever. I'd love to catch up with you and also let you know some things I've been working on that might be valuable for you. For instance, I've been showing other bakeries how they can reduce the number of outside resources they use. Give me a shout, and let's talk for five minutes. I'm at *<phone number>*."

―*᚜᚜᚜*―

The message I use is much more relationship-oriented and Right-Side Up. I might turn to LinkedIn for relationship fodder then leave a voicemail like the following:

―*᚜᚜᚜*―

YOU: "Hi, Yuri, this is *<your name, company and phone number>*. We haven't talked in forever and I saw on LinkedIn that you landed the role of Plant Manager at Sereus Dough. Wow! How did you snag that job? I totally want to hear the story. Let's catch up for ten minutes. Give me a call this evening at *<phone number>*. Or if that doesn't work, I'll be in tomorrow, too. I look forward to chatting."

―*᚜᚜᚜*―

Tips to Make Phone Outreach More Effective

- *Avoid gatekeepers by calling early in the morning or after 5:30 p.m.* when most assistants have left, but executives are still in their office. It's an old school tactic, but it still works.

- *Call five minutes* before *the hour*; i.e., 10:55 a.m. or 1:55 p.m. An executive who has a meeting scheduled for the top of an hour (which is common) will frequently be free about five minutes before the meeting starts. This is a great window to connect and use your Right-Side Up script. If they're in a hurry you can schedule a time to have a longer call.

- *It's okay to call just to touch base.* You don't have to have any grand reason in mind. You also don't have to have something extraordinarily meaningful to offer (contrary to popular belief). Simply connecting with someone nurtures the relationship and, therefore, is inherently valuable.

- *Don't skip anyone.* Sometimes it's tempting to only call the people you're comfortable reaching out to. Those folks are fair targets to start you rolling, but once you're in the groove, call the hard people, too.

- *Take notes immediately after the call*. Good note taking will make your next outreach much easier and more effective since you can reference key issues or events they talked about.

- *Remember to ask for introductions and remember to set the next date*. Did I mention those two practices will add at least 30% to your bottom line? I should have said at least 50%.

- *Above all, make that first call!* The first one is always the hardest, so put mechanisms or a ritual in place that will get you to pick up the phone that first time.

Effectively Nurturing Relationships in Person

Face-to-face meetings with prospects are, without a doubt, the richest, highest impact form of outreach. You are far more likely to surface a hot project opportunity during an in-person meeting than on the phone or via email. Plus, in-person meetings are better for building a bond. You get to see body language and you invariably share the sorts of personal connections that strengthen relationships.

Since time is a major drawback of in-person meetings, save this medium for your highest potential prospects. Always qualify prospects on the phone before meeting with them in person—even if it's someone you've known for a while.

The best candidates for in-person meetings are past clients, current clients and people who call with a specific project already in mind. Avoid in-person meetings with people who call out of the blue, want to "network" with you and suggest grabbing a coffee or lunch. Those can turn into huge time drains.

As I mentioned earlier, you can also schedule in-person meetings opportunistically. For instance, if you're traveling for a speech or a project, call your contacts in the city you're traveling to and book a couple of in-person sessions. Rick, the consultant I referenced in Chapter 5 who regularly sells more than $2 million in consulting each year, picks a city to travel to then calls all his contacts in that city and mentions that he "happens to be passing through" as an inducement to get an in-person meeting.

Rick's careful with his wording because he doesn't want prospects to feel pressured or obligated. When he can book five meetings in a single trip, it proves very productive. Of course, he's always making sure to meet with A1s and B1s—decision makers in every case.

I often run a breakfast meeting for consultants the day before or after I am scheduled to give a presentation in a distant city. Strictly speaking, if I'm presenting to 30 consultants over breakfast, it's not a one-on-one meeting, but I try to interact with each attendee to nurture individual relationships.

Finally, walking the halls, a tactic that was mentioned earlier, is also an effective one-on-one relationship nurturing tactic. Every time I'm at a client site I make a point to visit other executives I've already met. If at all possible, I sit down with each one for a five-minute conversation—longer, if we each have the time. Often we just have a quick catch-up conversation and connect on a personal level. On the other hand, it's not unusual that a new project opportunity pops up.

A Blast from the Past: Handwritten Notes

I didn't list handwritten letters or notes in Chapter 14's overview of outreach tactics because virtually no one uses them anymore, including me. (If you saw my handwriting, you'd know why.) However, if you have the handwriting and the discipline to use them, handwritten notes are relationship Miracle-Gro.

Ben, an airline consultant I know, keeps a dozen notecards in his briefcase at all times. Any time he's on a flight (which is at least once a week), he knocks out five or ten handwritten notes then drops them in the mail when he lands. His clients and contacts love him and feel a strong personal connection. After every meeting, he also sends a card to the key executives he met. It's a terrific touch and definitely helps Ben stand out from the crowd.

Creating and nurturing relationships are the keys to building a productive network. But at some point you need to leverage your contacts if you're going to win new business. How do you do it? Simple. You use The Turn.

BONUS MATERIAL

Bonus Materials available at davidafields.com/winningclients

David's Outreach Call Outline

CHAPTER 16

Leveraging Relationships

Most consultants would give their right arms to meet just a handful of the deci-sion makers Miranda knows. Seriously, if you had a spare limb (and who doesn't?), would you trade it for a list of personal relationships that makes the organizers of the World Economic Forum in Davos envious? Of course you would. Miranda, a consultant in Delaware has that list.

Her networking abilities are nothing short of stellar, and she could have easily written the last three chapters. Miranda works as a board-level consultant, which explains, in part, why the roster of people who will call her back is a who's who of big-name executives. Yet, for some reason her consulting business wasn't taking off.

After we worked together for a short while, we found out why. Although Miranda is an inveterate relationship creator and builder, she was devoting all her time to *nurturing* her relationships. She didn't know how to *leverage* those relationships into clients. When she integrated a new technique called "The Turn" into her approach, her consulting revenue blossomed.

Up to this point I've been talking a lot about *not* selling. I've hammered home Right-Side Up thinking, which puts your client's world first and subordinates your own interests. But wait a moment. Isn't this book supposed to help you *build* your consulting business? And if so, how do we reconcile such a relationship-oriented, low-pressure approach with winning more projects from more clients?

The answer? In many cases you won't need to reconcile relationship-building with rainmaking. Remember, while you've been nurturing your relationships, your contacts have been constantly reminded of your high impact, tightly focused offering, so when a problem arises that you can solve, they naturally reach out to you. *At least in theory.*

In practice, your clients are so focused on their own worlds that they often forget to call you even when they should. Therefore, you need to be more proactive about shifting the conversation to potential consulting engagements. How do you do it? Through a method I call "The Turn."

The Turn

The technique I'm about to show you is extraordinarily powerful. For many consultants, this one simple process totally transforms their practices. While it may look very elementary and even obvious in hindsight, The Turn is truly a game changer.

Before I detail how it works, let's review a problem you probably encounter on a daily basis. You're having a conversation with Yuri Yusimi, the plant manager at Sereus Dough, Inc., and it's all warm and friendly. Terrific. But you don't know how to transition the conversation to business and to discussing a possible project without sounding self-serving. It's uncomfortable. It's awkward.

IS THIS A PROPOSAL FOR *CONSULTING?*

There's a good reason for this awkwardness: you're running smack dab into the natural conflict between social behavior and market behavior. Daniel Ariely deftly explains the situation in his best-selling book, *Predictably Irrational*:

> *We live simultaneously in two different worlds—one where social norms prevail, and the other where market norms make the rules. The social norms include the friendly requests that people make of one another... Social norms are wrapped up in our social nature and our need for community. Reciprocity is not immediately required.*
>
> *The second world, the one governed by market norms, is very different. The exchanges are sharp-edged: wages, prices, rents, interest, and costs-and-benefits. Such market relationships ...imply comparable benefits and prompt payments.*
>
> *When we keep social norms and market norms on their separate paths, life hums along pretty well. When social and market norms collide, trouble sets in.*

The world of social norms is where relationship nurturing lives. The world of market norms is where asking-for-business lives. Therefore, it's not surprising that we feel anxious and disquieted about maneuvering a relationship-building conversation into business-building territory. The clash of norms can ruin your relationship and torpedo your chances of winning projects.

The solution to this war of the worlds is allowing them to be separate. That's where The Turn comes in. The Turn is a carefully constructed script that protects the warm, relationship norms while creating a space for market norms. It sounds like this:

YOU: "Would you be open to a separate conversation where we talk about your business, and explore whether my firm can help you achieve your goals?"

The absolutely critical components in that script are *separation* (i.e., talking about business in a different conversation) and *agency* (i.e., giving your prospect the choice). But there's more to the script than that. Figure 16-1 breaks down The Turn line by line:

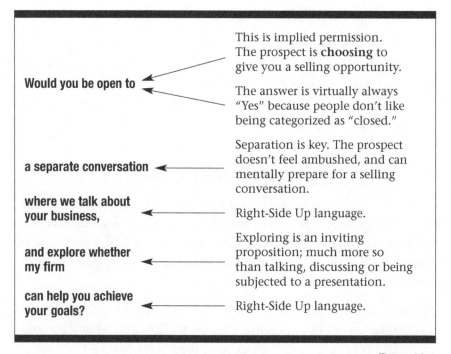

Figure 16-1

There are other ways to phrase The Turn that preserve the key elements of separation and agency, but the one I just outlined is consistently the most effective. If it just doesn't feel natural for you, then adapt it to fit your style. One consultant I work with says The Turn like this:

~~~~

YOU: "Yuri, many of the challenges you've mentioned are exactly the type of work we do for our clients. If at some point you'd be interested in discussing how we could work together on any of those, I would be delighted to have the conversation."

~~~~

The consultant preserves separation ("If at some point") and agency ("If ... you'd be interested"). Practice the script I've given you or your own version of The Turn until it's completely comfortable. It shouldn't take long because The Turn naturally bridges social and market norms.

Note that the separate conversation doesn't have to occur on a different day. Sometimes the prospect says, "Sure, let's talk about that now!" and you jump directly into Step 5: Become the Obvious Choice.

Targets for The Turn

You can use The Turn with any relationship, of course. However, it's most important that you practice it diligently with the decision makers on your contact list—these are the A1s and B1s, based on the network core segmentation exercise we went through together in Chapter 14.

Miranda's contact list was chock full of decision makers, and, as I said at the outset of the chapter, when she practiced The Turn with them her business trajectory experienced a major uplift.

When to Use The Turn

When do you use The Turn? *After* you've clearly demonstrated Right-Side Up thinking. Theodore Roosevelt (or his horse), summed it up perfectly:

Every well-established relationship that you've nurtured over many conversations is ripe for The Turn. That said, newer relationships could also be ready for The Turn if you've established Right-Side Up thinking. How long each connection takes depends on you, your contact, and how well and how quickly you hit it off.

I've met people and instantly built enough rapport that it's clear we can shift to business. With other people it might take two or three conversations before I attempt to leverage our new relationship.

Keep in mind that most relationship-building encounters with a new contact *won't include a discussion about potential project opportunities*. That's a perplexing statement for a consultant who feels that the only productive conversations are those that tie back to his consulting business.

It's much less confusing when you remember that your contact's important priorities often have nothing to do with you. Don't worry, a discussion that never touches on your business is okay! Talking about the issues pertinent to the prospect is part of the relationship nurturing process. But...

When your prospect raises a specific issue THAT MESHES WITH YOUR OFFERINGS, then it's time to employ The Turn.

The Best Medium for The Turn

You can use the script I've provided just about any way you communicate—in person, over the phone, during a video conference, and even over email. Email is my least favorite vehicle for The Turn because it's already a thin medium with dicey ability to convey emotions. Therefore, I only use The Turn in email if it's at the tail end of a conversation, and definitely not as part of an initial outreach message.

When The Turn Isn't Necessary

The Turn isn't always necessary. In fact, there are two common situations in which it's not needed at all.

1. ***When the prospect solicits your help***. If a contact reaches out to you for your services, don't say, "Hold on there, pal, let's do a bit more relationship building before we talk about working together." Instead, become the obvious choice (Step 5) and win a healthy project.

2. ***When the explicit purpose of your meeting is to discuss working together***. For instance, let's say Yuri Yusimi introduces you to his colleague, Mary. In his note to Mary, Yuri says, *"I'm introducing you to Bob at Topnotch Consulting. I think they might be able to help with that downtime issue on the Milwaukee line."*

   When you call Mary, she's expecting you to talk about a project opportunity even though you've never met her before. That's fine. The Turn isn't required. Just don't forget to nurture the relationship also.

Now that you've learned how to create and nurture your relationships, and how to gracefully leverage contacts into new business opportunities, it's time to transform those opportunities into slam dunks.

How do you do it? By discovering the hot buttons that will allow you to become the obvious choice. I love hot buttons! Let's find out what they are next.

Become the Obvious Choice

(Emerge as an Irresistible Solution)

Soon after mp3 players were invented, over 50 brands vied for market share. Consumers panned all of them. Noticeably absent was Apple, who patiently studied the market and emerging technology.

Then Apple introduced the iPod and dominated the industry for more than a decade.

—

"The obvious choice" is not an award bestowed upon you for rushing in with a whiz-bang proposal.

Rather, by being deliberate in your discovery, and by understanding your prospect better than anyone else, your simple solution will stand out above all others.

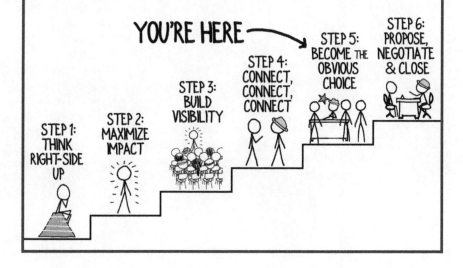

CHAPTER 17

How Clients Choose

By now, your confidence is soaring because you know your high-impact offer, you're visible to the executives who can hire you, and you're hooking their interest. Your professional network is burgeoning, and you're converting relationships into active prospects. And, of course, you're great looking, charming, and a gourmet chef.

Now the money will start pouring in, right?

Not exactly.

You need to uncover, client-by-client and project-by-project, what will make you an irresistible solution in the specific area you are targeting. **Becoming the obvious choice is rooted in the process of *discovery*.** The consultant who discovers better will understand the client better and know exactly how to grab the golden ring.

Think about the buying process for a board game, bottle of shampoo, antivirus software or other pre-packaged, shrink-wrapped product. The buyers realize they have a problem or aspiration (e.g., dirty hair or clean computer). They have some idea in mind of what they're looking for in a product. They scan the alternatives and finally buy the product that best meets their criteria.

WHICH CONSULTANT DO YOU
THINK WE SHOULD CHOOSE?

That's not our world. Consulting isn't about offering fixed, pre-packaged solutions. Consulting is about delivering situational, tailored, client-specific advice and outcomes. Even if you have a repeatable, scalable process, the output, analysis, insights, and recommendations are customized to each client.

The difference between the product world and our world is *huge*. If your offering is fixed, and static like a typical product, your odds of winning a project plummet.

Quite recently, a Washington D.C.-based company was looking for a consultant to help upgrade their go-to-market approach. They solicited proposals from a wide range of firms then narrowed the field down to two options: my firm and a consultancy headed by a well-known figure in the field whom I know and greatly respect. Ultimately, they chose my firm, and when I asked why, the decision maker said the other firm's rigid approach was good, but my plan fit them like a glove.

In typical product sales, once you capture a buyer's attention you're near the end of the buying process. The buyer evaluates you versus his need and plunks down some cash or chooses something else.

But in consulting, capturing a prospect's attention is the *beginning* of the process. Your hard work thinking Right-Side Up, maximizing impact, building visibility, and connecting collectively lead to the moment when a prospect says the magic words, *"I have a problem and I think you may be able to help."*

That's the moment you start the process of discovery that leads to a killer proposal they'll sign.

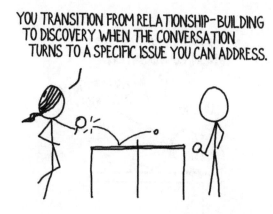

The moment your contact mentions a specific problem you can help solve is a point of opportunity. A real, live, potential project is on the line. But potential is not enough. To close the project you need to:

1. Maintain Momentum
2. Become the Obvious Choice

Maintaining Momentum

Once a lead stalls, it's usually (though not always) done. *Kaput.* Therefore, sustaining momentum while you're becoming the obvious choice is critical. The following technique will help you keep the process in motion until it flowers into a juicy project, or until you walk away to pursue a better prospect.

Always Lock In the Next Conversation

If I was asked to pick the one piece of advice most likely to double a consultant's revenue, it would be this: **Never, ever, finish a conversation with an active prospect without agreeing to the date and time for the next conversation.**

I mentioned this as a good practice to employ in your relationship-building discussions. Now that you have an interested prospect, the practice is critical.

From the moment you start discovery discussions until the point your prospect signs your contract, always nail down the date and time of the next conversation, *without exception*. It's actually a very easy technique and only requires you to be disciplined about using it every time.

Below is an example of how a conversation might flow.

━━━〰〰〰━━━

YOU: "Yuri, this conversation has been extremely helpful. If I get a summary of our discussion over to you by tomorrow, when would you be available to go through it? How does Wednesday afternoon look?"

YURI YUSIMI: "Uhm... I'm not sure how Wednesday afternoon is going to pan out. Why don't you send me the document and I'll give you a call by the end of the week."

YOU: "If you don't mind, let's try to get something on the calendar. I know how busy you get and my schedule gets pretty crazy too. So, it always seems to work better if we can find a time up front that works. How does Thursday at 9:00 a.m. work?"

YURI YUSIMI: "That should work. We'll talk then."

It's fairly common for prospects to resist your first attempt at nailing them down to a specific next time to talk. However, most prospects will pull out their calendars and agree to a date when you ask again and you bolster your request with a reason why it's important. A select few will require a bit more coaxing. Remember, it's okay to set a date even if the client doesn't expect to reach a decision by that date.

The only time I don't insist on locking in the specific next date and time is when the prospect is driving and talking on a mobile phone. In those cases I'll agree to reconnect when they stop driving and later that day we'll calendar our next conversation.

In addition to locking in the next conversation, the "Know Where You Stand" approach is a classic, highly effective momentum tool. You can download **The Know Where You Stand Momentum Tool** from the online resources.

Becoming the Obvious Choice

You're going to become the obvious choice by discovering what your prospects want, need, and value, then delivering solutions that fit them like a pair of comfy, old pajamas. That discovery process is depicted in detail in Chapters 18 and 19.

Before leaping in, though, I'm sure you want to understand how clients make decisions. In other words, what makes a prospect choose one consulting firm over another, or decide to work with internal staff rather than any consultant at all? Is it price? Is it experience? Is it a differentiated solution?

When you appreciate how clients choose, your discovery efforts will become much more effective and productive. When it comes to consulting projects, all clients' choices rest on the Six Pillars of Consulting Success.

The Six Pillars of Consulting Success

For you to win a consulting engagement, the Six Pillars of Consulting Success must be in place. *Every time you win a project, the six pillars are in place.*

They are:

1. Know   2. Like   3. Trust   4. Need   5. Want   6. Value

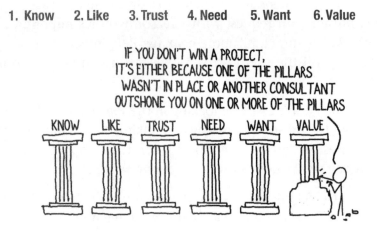

Know is your prospect's awareness of you. No consulting firm has ever won a project from a client who has never heard of them. The more well known you are, the greater the pool of prospective clients who could solicit your help on their pressing problems. Step 3: Build Visibility is all about becoming known.

Like is your prospect's impression of how pleasant working with you will be. Consulting is a human endeavor and when clients are considering a few consultants who are sufficiently skilled, they will choose the consultant with whom they experience the best rapport over a consultant who is objectively more qualified.

Trust is your prospect's belief, on a number of fronts, that you can be relied upon. We'll delve further into this pillar in a few minutes.

Need is your prospect's perception that a specific problem or aspiration must be addressed. It's the yawning gap between your prospect's views of how the world is and how the world *should* be.

Want is your prospect's *desire* to address specific problems or aspirations. It's the hunger that compels a client to take action. When proposals don't close for months on end, the problem is a lack of *Want*. Prospects frequently acknowledge there's a problem and agree the consultant can help resolve it, but then fail to take action. Action is scary. Change is scary. Therefore, for a project to close, the prospects' desire and urgency must outweigh their fears.

Value is your prospect's perception that engaging you will yield greater benefits than pursuing any other course with the same time and money. Some consultants mistakenly think *Value* is about ROI. It's usually not. Clients aren't comparing the return from your project to the cost. They're comparing the benefit of your project, financially and personally, to the benefit of doing something else. High *Value* makes for large, lucrative projects.

Know, *Need* and *Value* are the rational pillars. They're why a project exists and you're in the running to win it. *Like*, *Trust*, *Want*, and *Value* are the emotional pillars. They're why the project actually closes and you win it. As you can see, *Value* has both a rational and emotional component: "hard" benefits like profit and "soft" benefits like status or work-life balance.

While all six pillars are required to support a consulting sale, some carry more weight than others. The number one driver of choice is… (drumroll please)… *Trust*. This is true no matter what type of project you're working on, or what stripe of consultant you are.

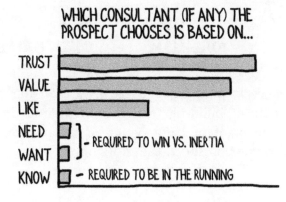

Figure 17-1

Clients choose the consultant they trust most.

The Trust Triangle—It's All About Me!

Entire books have been written to show you how to build trust. From a consultant's standpoint, though, trust is absolutely indispensable. It's also straightforward, and I'm going to shortcut the concept for you.

Trust is a triangle, and all three points of the triangle are about *me!* Except "me" in this case is from the prospect's perspective: you're considering me and have my best interests in mind, not just your own; you're going to help me by solving my problem; you're not going to hurt me by screwing up or making me look bad. The more a client believes you rock on all three points, the more he'll trust you.

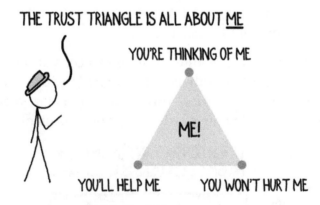

So, if the prospect's perspective is that trust is all about him, that means the core of building trust is... Right-Side Up thinking! (Thanks for blurting it out before you read it.) The more you listen and attend to your prospect, the more opportunity you have to build trust.

You should always strive to *be* trustworthy, of course. Then layer on your solid relationship, a dose of good listening, and provide the credibility boosters, risk reducers, project approaches, terms and structures that knock it out of the park on all three points of trust for that specific prospect.

For some prospects trust is built by demonstrating your years of experience in the industry, but others may want to know you're an industry outsider. One prospect may feel that adding extra analysts lowers the risk of missing a deadline, whereas another prospect may want fewer people on your team causing disruption.

What about testimonials, your pedigree, scorecards on previous projects and other contributors to credibility? You should absolutely develop all of those and keep them in your toolkit. However, remember that some prospects will be swayed by testimonials, whereas others may need more extensive evidence (e.g., a pilot project). It all depends. And that's why I'll reiterate: *discovery is your key to becoming the obvious choice.*

Who'd the Watchmaker Choose?

The CEO of a large watch manufacturer in New England told me he brought in a consultant on a major, multi-million-dollar engagement. The final three firms he considered were:

- Acme, a global firm he had worked with before that typically did a passable job;

- Breakthrough Group, a dynamic, innovative, boutique consulting firm that offered extremely aggressive (a.k.a. low) fees;

- ERP Associates a midsize firm that specialized in the watchmaker's exact issue.

The CEO chose Acme. Even though that consultancy wasn't the most experienced with his issue, or the least expensive, or the firm with the smartest people.

Dang, I wanted the boutique firm to win! But here's what the CEO told me about the decision: "David, I trusted that Acme could do the job. I'd worked with them before, and even though I knew they weren't the very best, I knew they could do it and wouldn't let me down."

That's the power of trust, and that's why building relationships and conducting the discovery process you'll learn in the next two chapters is imperative. To win the project with Yuri Yusimi at Sereus Dough, Inc., you don't have to be the best; you don't have to be the cheapest; you certainly don't have to be the biggest. *You have to be the consultant he trusts most.*

Beyond Trust: More Drivers of Choice

Below are other, influential factors involved in a client's selection of a consultant for his initiative. You'll quickly realize most of the factors interact in some way with *Trust* or *Value* or *Like*. The factors we'll cover quickly are:

- Situation Expertise
- Outcome Expertise
- Responsiveness
- Rapport
- Willingness to Push Back
- Project-Specific Criteria

Situation Expertise

The dominant question in a client's mind is, "Have you helped someone exactly like me with exactly the same problem?" You would think Yuri Yusimi would have all the baking industry expertise he needs already roaming the halls of Sereus Dough, but that's not how he sees it.

As a result, Yusimi (like most clients) first looks for consultants who have experience in his industry, with problems that look like the one he's trying to solve, and with companies that appear similar to

Sereus Dough. The consultant with the strongest credentials in those three areas will always be a front runner.

That's one reason an industry focus is so helpful to winning clients. If you're an expert in plasmatic node optimization, you can absolutely win consulting gigs in any industry that employs plasmatic nodes. However, if you and another consultant are equally adept at optimizing nodes *and* you have bakery industry expertise, you'll be Yusimi's obvious choice.

DO YOU HAVE EXPERIENCE IN THE DOUGH INDUSTRY?

I EAT A LOT OF PASTRIES. CLOSE ENOUGH

Outcome Expertise

"You will help me" is one of the three points on the Trust Triangle because that's at the root of what clients are looking for: a favorable outcome. Since many clients believe they know the best approach to solve their problem, they look for the consultant that is most facile in that approach. Nevertheless, if you can credibly tell a client, "I've solved your problem many, many times for companies exactly like yours using salted pistachios," he'll listen, even if your approach seems a little nuts.

Responsiveness

Being the most responsive consultant can absolutely win you a project. When a prospect calls three consultants and one calls back immediately and the others wait for a day or two, who do you think has a major leg up? Clients rightly assume that your responsiveness to them and their needs will be the same from the first contact through the final presentation. Nothing shows a client they're important as much as getting back to them promptly. And believe me, clients want to feel that they're the center of your world.

Rapport

Always keep in mind this is a human business. Clients prefer working with people they get along with and communicate with easily. The last thing an executive wants is to go home feeling angry or stressed out because of his consultant.

Willingness to Push Back

Few executives want to pay for an obse-quious consultant; they have plenty of sycophants walking around the office already. Carl, the division president of a large, transportation company was telling me about the knock-down-drag-out fights he had with a consultant on a very successful project. Carl said the consult-ant would never leave a meeting with him until they'd hammered out all their

I DIDN'T MEAN IT QUITE SO LITERALLY!

differences. He contrasted that to a failed project with a different con-sultant who had very little input and gave absolutely no push back.

Carl's message is *mostly* consistent with other clients I've inter-viewed. Most clients want you to act like a peer, not a vendor. Even clients who seem to want you to be subordinate appreciate your pushing back a bit if it makes them think and look better. Just don't make pushing back your most prominent attribute. Ultimately, clients want results, not more frustration. If you spend all your time arguing with them, they're going to give you the boot and find someone who will just get the job done.

Project-Specific Criteria

Often there are criteria that are unique to the client's particular proj-ect. Perhaps it's experience with a particular piece of equipment, or the need to have people on site, or a requirement that results be written in Swahili. For the most part, those criteria aren't the dif-ference between whether you or another consultant is chosen.

Rather, they determine whether you're even considered. If you meet the project requirements you're in the consideration set. If you don't, you're not.

But What About Your Unparalleled Approach?

You're justifiably proud of your innovative, unique, better-than-chocolate approach, right? After all, you've spent years perfecting it, and it's what separates you from all other consultants. Well, I've got news for you:

Differentiation doesn't matter in consulting. Results matter.

Make no mistake: your approach to delivering the client's outcome *is* pertinent. It will have a major bearing on whether he chooses you or chooses another consultant or whether he just sticks with his internal staff. But as I explained in Chapter 6, clients aren't looking for an approach that's different. They're looking for one that *works*.

Think of toothpaste. Toothpaste tubes were invented forever ago. Since then, manufacturers have invented squeeze bottles, pumps, sprays, drops, pills you put on your toothbrush and pretty much everything else. But what do you have in your bathroom at home? A toothpaste tube. It's easy to see how the tube works and it gets the job done. That's what your clients want: simple, easy and obvious. They want toothpaste tubes.

Trust. Got It. Now What?

By now, you know Yuri Yusimi will choose the consultant he trusts most; the one he believes is most likely to put him front and center; the one who will deliver the outcome he wants without hurting him along the way.

And I've told you that the marrow of building trust is discovery—listening carefully, actively, and with intent, then showing you understand your prospect deeply. But you may be thinking that you can't possibly win business by just letting your prospects ramble on about their problems. You're right. And wrong. Left to their own devices, prospects won't share the background data required for you to provide the most help.

However, truth be told, left to *your* own devices, you'll jump into strutting your stuff too early, and you won't ask for the right information—or the "Irony of Expertise" will kick in and you'll jump to conclusions about what the problem is and how to solve it. To avoid all these issues, irresistible consultants rely on the Context Discussion. As you're about to see, it's the centerpiece of building trust and, ultimately, becoming the obvious choice.

BONUS MATERIAL

Bonus Materials available at davidafields.com/winningclients

The Know Where You Stand Momentum Tool

CHAPTER 18

Discovering
Context—Part 1

The heart and soul of Becoming the Obvious Choice is what I call the Context Discussion. Developing the Context Discussion was one of the big breakthroughs in my own consulting career, and I've seen many other consultants make similar breakthroughs using it. When you master this conversation, you will increase your close rate and shorten your sales cycle. And I mean *dramatically*.

What is the Context Discussion? It's a carefully constructed approach to discovery, and it is the single, most important conversation (or set of conversations) paving the way to unlimited clients and financial freedom.

The Context Discussion reminds me of the Jewish holiday of Passover. On Passover, children chant the "four questions." The same questions in the same order, every time, at every Passover Seder, everywhere in the world. The Context Discussion is like that, only it's the "six topics."

A quick warning, though: don't jump into the Context Discussion too soon. You can sour a relationship and lose millions of dollars of business by rushing into discovery before your prospect is ready. How do you know if it's time for a Context Discussion? One of two ways:

1. A prospect contacts you out of the blue because of your visibility-building efforts (a.k.a. marketing) and solicits your help.

2. During a relationship-building conversation you surface a *specific* problem or aspiration you could help address and then, using The Turn, you secure permission to explore the opportunity.

In both cases, you now have an "active prospect" and your job is to position yourself to close the project.

The Power of the Context Discussion

When Isaac, a senior executive at Pine Tree Bank, was about to embark on a major project, he was pointed my way by Stan, a mutual acquaintance. To Isaac's credit, when he called, he told me he had already interviewed other consultants and had most likely selected a winner. He was only speaking to me at Stan's suggestion. Unfazed, I asked him whether he would be willing to answer some questions. Of course, he agreed. What he didn't know was that my Socratic approach was expertly designed to build trust and win the project.

WHEN YOU CREATE A SAFE SPACE FOR PROSPECTS TO BE VULNERABLE (AND DO SO IN A HELPFUL AND NON-MANIPULATIVE WAY), THEY'LL START TO TRUST YOU.

WOW!

I didn't break out the hackneyed questions like, *What are your objectives?* Or the storied, *"five whys."* Those queries won't get you very far. They don't coax the prospect to open up and share some of his innermost thoughts with you. Instead, I used a series of inquiries that framed and focused Isaac's issues in ways he'd never considered in depth, or, in many cases, never considered at all.

I followed up our conversation with the Context Document and, two days later, Isaac told me, "I absolutely believe that you can deliver on what we need." Even though Isaac had a consultant in mind before I waltzed into the party at the eleventh hour, he chose me. And, by the way, we signed a contract for 55 percent more than he had originally budgeted.

The reason I won Isaac's project is simple: the Context Discussion. Over the course of that conversation, he started to think, *"This guy really understands me."* At that point, the project was in the bag.

A Roadmap of the Context Discussion

The Context Discussion is a conversation that covers six specific topics. If you've ever found yourself in long, meandering, introductory conversations with prospects, those days are gone. By covering the same six topics in roughly the same order every time, you'll have a roadmap to guide you crisply through the inquiry process. You and your prospects (soon to be clients) will both be much happier.

Tell your prospect at the outset that you'd like to cover six topics. This previews where you're headed and demonstrates from the start that you have a robust process. Simply knowing you're being deliberate starts to create a safe space for him to share. The six topics you're going to cover are:

1. Situation
2. Desired Outcomes
3. Indicators of Success
4. Perceived Risks and Concerns
5. Value
6. Parameters

These six topics provide deep insight into your prospect's current situation and desired future. You both benefit from this discovery process, and that's why the exact process I'm detailing for you now is the same one I recommend to my corporate clients (I wrote about it in Chapter 3 of *The Executive's Guide to Consultants*).

The Platinum Rule

The inviolable, platinum rule of Context Discussions is that, sooner or later, they *must* be conducted with the decision maker or decision makers. Can you conduct this discussion at other levels of the organization? Absolutely. Does that discovery substitute for the discussion you need to have with the ultimate decision maker? Absolutely not.

No matter how many people you conduct discovery with along the way, you must also cover all six Context Discussion topics with the decision maker.

The Context Discussion could last thirty minutes with one individual, or it could span thirty days with a range of influencers before it concludes with the decision maker. Of course, it's not practical to include full-blown discovery conversations in a book of this length, but I think you'll get the idea from the vignettes below.

From here on out, *everything I tell you and all the examples are going to assume you are talking to the decision maker*. Even though your words will change from situation to situation, the principles apply to every active prospect.

For the purpose of illustration let's make that decision maker our friend Yuri Yusimi from Sereus Dough, Inc. He happens to have an operations-related problem, but the exact same conversation works for any consultant, advising clients on any topic. And for ease of understanding, Bob, from TopNotch Consulting, will take your place as the consultant in these examples.

1. Situation

The first part of your discussion investigates why the prospect is looking for assistance. Prospects are usually willing to talk quite a lot about this, and part of your challenge is focusing them on the precise information you need. Here's how the Situation portion of the Context Discussion flows:

—*mm*—

YURI YUSIMI: "Thanks for coming in, Bob."

BOB: "My pleasure, Yuri. How can I help you?"

YURI YUSIMI: "Well, we have a handful of croissant manufacturing lines that are not meeting the targeted requirements. We've been trying to improve the performance, but we don't seem to be able to push it any higher on any of these lines."

BOB: "Okay, so you seem to have hit some limits. If you don't mind me asking, why are you focusing on the performance of the croissant lines?"

YURI YUSIMI: "Well, I have some extremely high performance objectives, and unless I get this equipment operating at a higher level, I don't see any chance of hitting those objectives. If I miss the objectives, we lose a heck of a lot of money. It could also put our bagel launch in jeopardy."

BOB: "Got it. It sounds like those flaky croissants lines are on the critical path for a number of important initiatives."

YURI YUSIMI: "Absolutely. We have to get the performance up. Here's what I think we need. In the Ohio plant we're seeing really long downtime because some spare parts aren't available. I'd like you to look at the repair loop on that equipment. And on the Milwaukee lines I'd like you to run an analysis of all the flour—"

BOB: [interjecting] "I'm sorry to interrupt, Yuri, but before we get to that level, do you mind if I ask a question?"

YURI YUSIMI: "Sure. What, Bob?"

BOB: "What's changed? I mean, I hear that you've hit a performance limit on the croissant lines, but I'm guessing you've been

at or near these limits for quite a while. What's happened that makes you want to exceed those limits now?"

YURI YUSIMI: "Well, I've wanted to exceed those limits all year. You're right that we've been bumping up against them for a while. What's changed? Hmm… I think that we've just hit a level of complexity and knowledge that's beyond my internal team. They've captured the low-hanging fruit, but we've got to look at the problems a different way or I'm never going to hit my targets."

BOB: "Okay, so would it be fair to say that what's changed is you've come to the realization that your internal teams won't be able to make further progress, and also that you've realized you need to act now or you'll miss your targets?"

YURI YUSIMI: "Yeah, I think that's fair."

BOB: "Great. It sounds like your teams have been looking at these manufacturing lines for a while. What have they done so far?"

YURI YUSIMI: "Good question. You should probably check with Reggie, the head of engineering to get the details, but I'll give you the parts I know and understand. They've conducted an assessment of the throughput rates and looked for mismatches on the interplasmatic buttering nodes…" *(Yusimi continues to share)* "… and that's what I know. As I said, I'd like you to meet with Reggie to get more details."

BOB: "Thanks. That was terrific information, and I'll definitely meet with Reggie as we dig into this further. I think I know the answer to this next question because you've already talked about it, but I want to check. Given the strength of your internal teams, why are you turning to the outside? Why call in my firm?"

YURI YUSIMI: "That's a fair question. My guys are good. I think they're the best in the company, if not the industry. But let's be realistic. They simply don't have the knowledge of this stuff that you do. They've gone as far as they can go, but to get the final five to ten percent of performance on croissants we're going to need the depth of expertise that you have and we don't."

BOB: "Thanks, that's very helpful."

Let's break down what Bob covered with his prospect. First, Yusimi offered some information about the bigger picture, and Bob inquired to learn more. The idea here is to learn how the project at hand fits in strategically with what the company is doing. This is typically pretty easy information to obtain, and the prospect is happy to share it.

Then, when Yusimi started talking about what he needed, Bob slowed him down a little bit and asked a crucial question: *"What's changed?"* The objective at this point is to discover the catalyst that's driving this project. Why are they doing the project now rather than last year or a year from now? Some events must have led to the prospect's desire for this project. What's happened or changed that suddenly makes this project important? Did a tool fail? Were new budgets set? Is there a review meeting coming up?

**There is ALWAYS a catalytic event
and you need to uncover it.**

The catalyst is also going to give you clues about the emotional drivers—the *Want* that is creating urgency—and will help you close the project. Often, when you uncover the catalytic event, you realize your prospect's original request—the project he talked about when he first contacted you—was heading in the wrong direction. This is an excellent chance to reframe the prospect's thinking.

Reframing is an exceptionally potent complement to listening. You reframe by fundamentally shifting your prospect's outlook, understanding of his situation, or perception of his needs. By creating this shift you demonstrate that you understand your prospect deeply and that you have a remarkable command of the issues at hand.

For instance, Bob could have suggested that Yusimi's root problem isn't the throughput rates on the croissant line. Then Bob could have raised the larger, more important concern that Yusimi's engineers aren't able to handle complex, operational issues. Reframing like this changes the very nature of the project. It knocks other consulting firms out of the box if you were in a competitive situation, and sets you up for a richer, higher-impact engagement.

After Bob knew the catalyst for the project, he asked what Yusimi had already done. In other words, what decisions have been made already, based either on evidence or strategy or, sometimes, nothing at all, and what needed to be tackled now?

Finally, Bob asked why Yusimi was turning to the outside. A lot of consultants forget to ask this question or they shy away from it. Maybe they're afraid the prospect is going to say, "*Hmmm... you know what? That's a good question. Why am I turning to a consultant? Maybe I can just do this myself. Thanks for coming in!*"

Any prospect who's that easily deterred from hiring a consultant would realize he doesn't want a consultant before signing a project anyway. So, if you ask, "*Why do you need a consultant?*" and the prospect answers, "*You know what, I don't!*" then you have just saved yourself a lot of grief and heartache.

The truth is, that rarely happens. In fact, what usually happens is the client starts justifying why he needs to bring in outside help. And how awesome is that?

IT'S A LOT EASIER TO WIN A PROJECT WHEN THE PROSPECT IS CONVINCING YOU THAN WHEN YOU'RE CONVINCING THE PROSPECT.

2. Desired Outcomes

Now let's see how the Desired Outcomes portion of the conversation between Bob and Yuri Yusimi unfolds:

BOB: "Thanks, that's very helpful. I know you've said you want to improve the performance of the croissant lines. *What's the ultimate outcome you are hoping for from this initiative?*"

YURI YUSIMI: "Good question. I really want you to focus on the Ohio lines and look at the repair loop on that equipment. I'd also like to see an analysis of all the flour sifters in the Milwaukee plant."

BOB: "Okay. I think I may have asked the wrong question. What I'm trying to find out is what your expectations are for how you'll actually be better off at the end of the project. What will be different then versus where you are now?"

YURI YUSIMI: "Oh. Well, I'm hoping that at the end we're going to have better croissant throughput and lower changeover times."

BOB: "Great. I think those are good outcomes. And if we improve throughput and lower changeover times, then what? How are you better off?"

YURI YUSIMI: "I'm better off because I'll be able to hit my performance targets… and I'll be better off because if I hit my performance targets, I'm going to get a good bonus, and you and I will go out for a drink!"

BOB: "Sounds good to me! If we enable you to hit your performance targets, then this project will have been a success. Right?"

YURI YUSIMI: "Unquestionably."

—*mm*—

You're probably very familiar with the part of the discussion we just went through. It's establishing the objectives for the project. While you're there, strive to unearth the highest value outcome rather than accepting, unchallenged, the initial outcome your prospect presents. To help you in this quest, you can download **25 Questions that Uncover Higher Value Projects.**

Rather than diving deeply into Desired Outcomes, you may decide to keep this section brief. That's a fine decision, but don't gloss over the Desired Outcomes section too quickly. I know how tempting it is to go along with whatever the prospect asks for—especially if he raises a problem you're expert in solving! However, prospects often have the wrong outcome in mind, and that can lead to an unsatisfying project with underwhelming results.

You may also have noticed that Bob pressed hard to understand how the client would be better off at the end of the project. Most clients want to talk about "deliverables" and, in my experience, most consultants want to talk about them, too. Dig deeper. Find the *outcome* that will delight the client.

DELIVERABLES DON'T INHERENTLY HAVE VALUE. OUTCOMES HAVE VALUE.

3. Indicators of Success

Once you've established your prospect's desired outcome, the discussion should turn to Indicators of Success. Let's observe this part of the Context Discussion in action.

━━━〰〰〰━━━

BOB: "Fair enough. The outcome, then, is hitting the performance targets on the croissant lines." (*Yusimi nods approval*). "The next question deals with how we measure success. How will you know if the project has been successful?"

YURI YUSIMI: "Well, if I hit my performance targets, then we'll know!"

BOB: "Right. I get that. And what would the performance targets be?"

YURI YUSIMI: "I'd have to look up the specific numbers on these lines. But, if I've achieved a certain throughput by the end of the year, then my plant is operating profitably. Oh, and I make a nice bonus."

BOB: "Okay, so ultimately we're looking at the performance of the croissant lines against the targets that you have set for the year, and you can send those to me later. That sounds like a lagging indicator, though. We won't know whether we've hit the mark until the year is done."

YURI YUSIMI: "That's true. You're right about that."

BOB: "So, what would some leading indicators be? How would we know that we're on the right track during the project?"

YURI YUSIMI: "Uhm... I think we should be looking at maintenance time, and probably line consistency. Those will give us a good idea of whether the performance targets are within reach."

BOB: "Perfect. What would a successful reduction in maintenance time be, and what does good croissant consistency look like?"

YURI YUSIMI: "If we can get maintenance time down 25 percent over the next six months, I'd be ecstatic. And, let's see... on average, the line consistency is at 68 percent now. If I want to achieve my performance targets, we'll need to get that to 73 percent."

BOB: "Okay, so if we get the maintenance time down 25 percent and the consistency up five points, you're going to be a happy client?"

YURI YUSIMI: "Very. I'll be a thrilled client."

—*mm*—

Bob's queries were pretty straightforward. Though, of course, in a real life situation you would probe more and for longer. Bob addressed one, basic subject that is going to help in many, many ways: how will he and Yusimi know when they have achieved Yusimi's desired outcome?

There are numerous ways to request this information: "What metrics can we put in place so that we know if we're making progress toward the success?" Or, "Yuri, if you're trying to get from A—where you are now—over here to B, how will you know when you get there?"

Establishing indicators of success starts making the benefits of the project more concrete for your client. He starts picturing success and feeling it. And, as we know, that creates *Want*, which is one of the Six Pillars of Consulting Success.

Let's move on to what may be the most critical element of all: *Perceived Risks and Concerns*. This section of the Context Discussion builds trust and sets the table for a stress-free close. Sounds pretty important, doesn't it? It is.

BONUS MATERIAL

Bonus Materials available at davidafields.com/winningclients

25 Questions that Uncover Higher Value Projects

CHAPTER 19

Discovering
Context—Part 2

Can you imagine walking into a job interview and asking, "So, what are all the things that could go wrong if you hired me?" That would be crazy, right? Yet, even though that's an ill-advised question if you're looking for employment, it turns out to be exactly the right line of inquiry when you're trying to win consulting projects.

Most consultants nervously attempt to skirt their prospects' worries. You, on the other hand, are going to consistently unmask your prospect's apprehensions and, by doing so, trigger a deeper conversation and win a greater level of respect and trust. It immediately separates you from the pack.

Asking about risks and concerns is a key ingredient in my secret sauce. It transformed my practice, and it's spurred a quantum leap in performance for many consultants I've worked with too.

To see how it works, let's watch the conversation deepen as the Context Discussion continues between Bob, who's standing in for you, and our prospect, Yuri Yusimi from Sereus Dough, Inc.

4. Perceived Risks and Concerns

We'll pick up the conversation where we left off in the last chapter...

—*mm*—

BOB: "That's what I like to hear. But as you think about the work we're discussing, what do you see as the key risks and what are your concerns about doing this project?"

YURI YUSIMI: "My biggest concern? Hmm. It's that we don't hit the targets. Making these numbers is what my bonus is based on, and if I don't get the croissant line up to where it should be, I don't see how I have a chance."

BOB: "Anything else?"

YURI YUSIMI: "Well, of course, I'm concerned about how long this is going to take. How long do these projects typically take?"

BOB: "Okay, I hear another concern is timing. I have absolutely no clue about that yet. We're still figuring out what the whole project is, but if I can ask a few more questions, then I can probably at least give you a very rough range on timing. Would that be okay?"

YURI YUSIMI: "Sure. Of course."

BOB: "Good. So hitting the numbers and the timing. Any other concerns? What about bringing in an outsider like us? Any worries about that?"

YURI YUSIMI: "Well, of course, I do have some concerns about how my engineering team is going to react. They've been working on croissants a long time and I don't want them to feel as though I don't trust them. So, we'll have to find a way to make this a win for them."

BOB: "Absolutely. That's a very fair issue. We see that all the time. Anything else?"

—*mm*—

Even though that was a condensed version of what would happen in an actual conversation, you still saw Bob ask Yusimi a couple of questions you may never have thought to ask before. Or, even if you thought about it, you may have been reluctant to ask.

The very thought of asking Yusimi his concerns about working with you might scrunch your face up like curdled milk. Unscrunch, because these questions are your secret passage to the land of closed projects. They're a breakthrough.

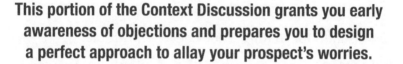

This portion of the Context Discussion grants you early awareness of objections and prepares you to design a perfect approach to allay your prospect's worries.

When you ask, "Yuri, what worries you?" it shows that you're interested and you care. Plus, when prospects share their fears, they're expressing vulnerability. Your interest and their vulnerability add up to a very quick path to *Trust* which, as we know from Chapter 15, is the five hundred pound gorilla in the fight to win consulting projects.

Resist your desperate urge to bust out intelligent answers or case studies in response to your prospect's concerns. That would shift the focus of the conversation to you, and right now your job is to stay wholly focused on your prospect.

In later discussions and in your proposal you'll be able to address their worries. When you do, you'll be perceived as one of those rare, desirable people who understands them deeply and pays attention to their concerns. That, my friend, is an extraordinarily powerful place to be.

5. Value

Let's move to the next part of the Context Discussion, which investigates the expected Value of the project.

—*mm*—

BOB: "Thanks for sharing those concerns with me."

YURI YUSIMI: "No problem; that was interesting. I'm glad you asked."

BOB: "Yeah, it's always an interesting discussion. My next question, though, is: why bother? I mean, I get that you want to hit these targets, and that will allow you to meet your performance targets for the year. But, in real terms, what does that mean for you?"

(At this point, Bob spends time helping Yuri Yusimi think through the value of his project. Like most prospects, Yusimi hasn't given it much thought. Also, since some of the benefits aren't concrete and don't immediately tie to sales or profit, Bob has to guide the thought process to create a concrete estimate Yusimi believes in.)

BOB: "So, let's work with the low end of your estimate. If we can get croissant throughput up and maintenance times down, that looks to be about six million dollars over three years. Does that seem like a fair estimate?"

YURI YUSIMI: "Yeah. I think that might be low, but that's fair."

BOB: "What else is required to achieve all this value we just uncovered? Surely this project alone won't get you there."

YURI YUSIMI: "Oh, well, we would also have to do some training and probably put in a new scheduling system."

BOB: "Okay, so maybe this project only delivers half of that six million. Does that sound reasonable?"

YURI YUSIMI: "Yeah. That makes sense."

BOB: "Okay, and what if you didn't bring in a consultant like us? Your engineers are smart and could probably make some progress on their own."

YURI YUSIMI: "Oh, my team is very good, Bob, but to be honest, we've already worked on this for six months without making progress. I think we've reached the limit of our internal capabilities."

BOB: "Okay, but let's be conservative and assume your guys could chip away at it, and the value of bringing in a consultant is about fifty percent. One more question: What do you think the likelihood is that this project will succeed? I've been doing this a long time and I know that even though we're the best in the business, not every project succeeds. What's your honest guess on how likely you think it is that we'll reach a successful conclusion?"

YURI YUSIMI: "I'm not entirely sure. No one's asked me that before. What do you think?"

BOB: "Our success rate is close to 100 percent. But to be conservative, I'm going to factor in a 20 percent chance we don't succeed. Now, let's see..."

Bob quickly calculates the value based on the factors he and Yusimi discussed:

$6 million over three years

x 50% for the project's contribution to the goal

x 50% for the consultant's contribution

x 80% estimated likelihood of success

$1.2 million risk-adjusted value.

BOB: "Based on your numbers, the risk-adjusted value of this project is $1.2 million. That's not my fee for the project, of course! It's not even the total benefit you'll receive from a successful project—when we succeed, the total gain is six million. But the value of bringing us in to do this project is $1.2 million. That will help you evaluate whether this project is a good investment."

YURI YUSIMI: "Oh. I see. That makes sense. I'd never thought of that before. That really helps."

—*mm*—

This approach to the Value discussion may seem complex, but I assure you 95 percent of prospects love it and it sets you apart from other consultants. You'll become good at it with a bit of practice.

Many consultants are afraid of digging into Value because they're afraid the prospect might say, *"Now that I think about it, this project isn't worth doing."* I've also seen consultants completely avoid the Value questions because they bring up the whole scary issue of money. Set those fears aside. The Value section of the Context Discussion is absolutely critical and if you don't do it now, you're going to struggle to close the project later.

To help you work your way through the Value questions, I've made a couple of bonus resources available to you on my website: **37 Common Sources of Value**, and **The Value Discussion Questions**.

Remember, when it comes to quantitative valuations, you need your prospect to provide the figures! This is not a place where you, the consultant, are creating all the numbers. Be a guide, but ultimately the client has to determine the value. (By the way, that means you can't make it up after the conversation is over. I've seen that plenty of times, and it doesn't work.)

Finally, before you tie a bow on your estimate of Yusimi's financial gain (or other concrete benefit), pursue one more line of inquiry. It sounds like the dialogue below:

—*mm*—

BOB: "Great. One more question. We've estimated what you might gain. But tell me, what does it cost you if you don't improve the croissant line?"

YURI YUSIMI: "Well, we'd lose that six million dollar upside."

BOB: "Okay, but do you believe that? What do you think is really at risk?"

YURI YUSIMI: "Uhm... the problem is we lose any chance to expand the croissant business. Over the long run, that's much bigger than the dollars we've been talking about."

—*mm*—

Bob asked a variation of: What does it *cost* you if you don't do this project? The word "cost" is extremely important, for two reasons:

1. Avoiding losses is a stronger motivator for most people than potential gain;

2. Cost is always at the front of our prospects' minds. Since Yusimi's concerned with the cost of the project you want to frame value in those terms too.

Don't Forget the Emotional Benefits

Let's talk about soft benefits for a moment. Soft benefits—the emotional benefits to the client for doing this project you're discussing—are easily as important as any pecuniary gain. In fact, they're often *more* important.

The rational *Need* and *Value* pillars must be in place to justify a project, but the *Want* and emotional *Value* pillars compel your prospect to act; i.e., hire a consultant. I usually use a very simple question to politely dig into emotional gain…

—⁓⁓—

BOB: "Okay, I get the financial reasons for doing this project. But how will success on this project help you, personally, Yuri?"

YURI YUSIMI: "Huh. Well, I'll make my bonus, of course, and that will be nice. But this croissant line has been a particular thorn in my side and as much as I'd like to be considered for a VP spot, I don't think there's any chance until I get croissants straightened out. So, this is critical to my career at Sereus."

—⁓⁓—

A couple of things to keep in mind during the Value part of the discussion: First, err on the side of conservatism. Second, be as concrete as possible. Nail down the specific pieces that add to the value and work out the math with your clients so that they can see it. On the emotional side, or soft benefits side, paint a vivid picture of the benefits.

6. Parameters

Now let's turn to the final section of the Context Discussion: timing, budget, people, and other issues that will affect the scope and your approach.

—*mm*—

BOB: "Okay, we're almost done. Just one more topic, and it's around parameters. I usually think of a project's parameters in three ways: people, time, and money. Are there any people issues we need to keep in mind? You brought up the engineering group. Is there anyone else that should be involved, or should be excluded, or that we need to watch out for?"

YURI YUSIMI: "Well... I think you have a meeting set up after this one to talk with the people involved on the croissant lines. They're the right people to talk with, so, I think we're okay on that."

BOB: "Great. And what about time? Are there any timing issues we should be keeping in mind?"

YURI YUSIMI: "Yes. This all has to create results by the end of the year because that's when the performance targets are reviewed."

BOB: "Perfect. I've made a note of that. Finally, are there money or cost issues I need to keep in mind? Cash flow, for instance, or signing authority limits that will affect this?"

YURI YUSIMI: "There always are. We definitely need to keep the costs down on this. Procurement's going to be pressing you pretty hard—they report directly into corporate. But overall, I have to make sure the cost is low and I get a good ROI."

BOB: "Well, based on the value numbers we agreed on a few minutes ago, giving you an outstanding ROI shouldn't be a problem. You've brought up keeping the cost down a couple of times now. Is there a number you have in mind or a limit we need to stay below?"

YURI YUSIMI: "No. I don't have a number in mind. As long as you deliver the results, and the fees are low enough that we get a good ROI, that should be fine."

BOB: "I totally get it. Thanks. Let me summarize what we've covered..."

—*mm*—

In this final part of the conversation, Bob quickly walked his prospect through common issues that can affect the scope of a project. I usually lead with people, time, and money, but also include geography, or language requirements, or anything else that seems appropriate. (Access to fresh croissants off the line, for instance. Just sayin'.)

While timing parameters are fairly common, the client doesn't always think them through, which is one of the reasons you're going to investigate it now. Mid-project is not the time to find out there was a deadline and you're late!

Finally, there's the money issue. Money is always a touchy subject when it comes to consulting projects, and many consultants are afraid to bring the topic up. Don't be. The prospect is thinking about it, and it's better to get the discussion out there on the table. The two biggest money parameters tend to be budget limitations and cash flow. If either one is a factor, try to understand the challenge early in the process.

If your prospect is reluctant to tell you his budget, gently press a little bit. Sometimes I'll test for an upper range using something like the following:

~~~

BOB: "I haven't thought through the fees yet, obviously, but I don't want to come back with something that's totally out of the question. What number would give you guys an absolute heart attack?"

YURI YUSIMI: (laughing) "Well, I'm not sure, but I can tell you anything over $300,000 would definitely give my boss a heart attack! It needs to come in much lower than that, though."

~~~

Just like that you've allowed the prospect to set a high, reference price and you've discovered a top end that can anchor your thinking on fees.

What is Not Covered in the Context Discussion

- The detailed approach or process you'll propose
- The number of consultants and analysts on the project
- How you're going to interact with the client
- Project fees
- Contract structures
- Pretty much everything else

Those pieces are important down the road, but they can be tabled until Yusimi agrees to the Context.

If it feels like the Context Discussion is a lot of effort, you're partly right. It can be. The Context Discussion can take numerous repetitions to master, and with some clients it can take weeks of conversations to fully work your way through the process. But even as you're learning this approach, you'll experience an immediate improvement in your business development results. And often the Context Discussion is quite easy.

With some clients, I've run through all six topics in only 40 minutes on the way to winning a six-figure project. The Context Discussion does the heavy lifting and lays much of the foundation for your success. It's the core of your new business efforts.

But here's the gooey, cherry center in the chocolate: you've just learned everything you need to know to become the obvious choice! You know what your prospect wants, what he needs, what could go wrong, who's involved, what bounds the project... everything.

That's why the discovery process you just learned makes it so easy to dance through the final step. You're on the verge of winning an engagement. It's time to propose, negotiate and close the project.

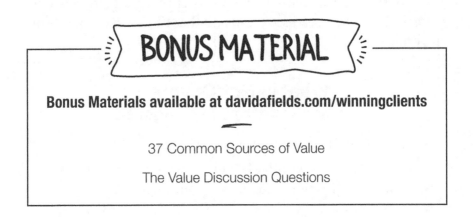

BONUS MATERIAL

Bonus Materials available at davidafields.com/winningclients

37 Common Sources of Value

The Value Discussion Questions

Propose, Negotiate & Close

(Enjoy the Payoff)

The Phyllostachys moso bamboo patiently
builds its root network over a period of years.

Then it shoots from a seedling to a towering, productive,
long-lasting, twenty-foot-tall tree... in only three weeks.
Growth so explosive and quick, it almost defies belief.

After deliberately finding the most fertile target, building your presence,
nurturing relationships and focusing on your prospects' context,
you'll find your practice skyrocketing to new heights.

Larger and more enduring client relationships appear faster
than you could have thought possible.

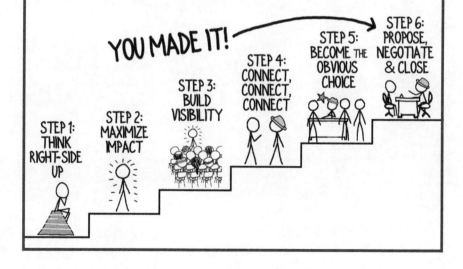

CHAPTER 20

Setting Up the Close

You've made it. You've reached the final stage where all your diligent efforts pay off. Now it's time to close some deals and get to work doing what you like to do most: helping clients overcome their problems and achieve their aspirations.

Closing projects is fun. It feels great, and we all want to close more projects more often. Why don't we? It's really quite simple. Most consultants have either forgotten or don't understand the key to closing success:

Closing isn't something you do.
Closing is the result of everything you've already done.

Let's say you stop at a farm stand where there's a stack of mouth-watering, homemade peach pies on display. You notice the farmer nearby and call out to him, "Hey, how did you get such sweet, succulent peaches for these pies?" The farmer replies, "Well, son, about five years ago I selected a strain of peach trees that would produce the finest fruit under the right conditions. I measured the acidity of my loam..." and then he waxes poetic about how he tended the soil and fertilized the tree and attracted the right type of butterfly.

Closing consulting projects is much the same. It might look like you wander to that prospect over yonder and pluck a juicy project. But really it's the five years or five months of attracting the Right People, then fertilizing and tending relationships that produce ripe opportunities. Then you mix all the ingredients in the proper order before, finally, placing a proposal in the oven, er, submitting your proposal to your prospect.

The Crux of Closing

I can't emphasize enough that the main ingredient in closing new projects—where the alchemy occurs that will catapult you to world-class close rates—is the Context Discussion. It's during the Context Discussion that you uncover the *Need* and quantitative *Value* that justify the project. Plus you expose the *Want* and soft *Value* that are the emotional kickers behind the initiative.

The portion of the Context Discussion that focuses on perceived risks and concerns is twenty-four-karat gold. At the end of the sales process, when most consultants are wrestling with objections, you're home free. You'll have used the insight you gathered during the Context Discussion to construct a proposal with an approach and contract structure that mitigate your prospect's concerns. As a result, objections melt away before they ever come up for negotiation.

So, if you haven't mastered the Context Discussion, go back and review it a few times. Practice it. Get help learning the nuances if you need to. The more adept you are at becoming the obvious choice, the more fun and the greater success you're going to have in proposing, negotiating, and closing.

The Two-Stage Proposal Process

Remember those peach pies? (I sure do. Yum.) Their scrumptious, flaky crusts are the result of mixing the dry ingredients and butter before drizzling in the water. It's a two-stage process that takes a bit of patience. But what a payoff! You're going to follow two stages also.

Stage 1 is explicitly confirming the Context. During this stage you're also going to start crafting and revealing your persuasive story.

Stage 2 is adding the final components that comprise a killer proposal, then submitting it for approval.

Stage 1: Agreement to the Context

The next, very important step after you conduct a Context Discussion is to summarize the highlights of your discovery conversations in a document called... wait for it... the Context Document. (Creative, right?) As a reminder, the six stages of the Context Discussion that you're going to recap in the Context Document are:

1. Situation
2. Desired Outcomes
3. Indicators of Success
4. Perceived Risks and Concerns
5. Value
6. Parameters

Your Persuasive Story

There's more to a Context Document than summarizing the discovery conversations on a few pages and dashing them off to Yusimi. This is where you start crafting the persuasive story that's going to win over Yusimi's heart and wallet.

Hiring a consultant is an emotion-laden act for prospects. They're committing themselves and putting themselves at risk. That's why you need to woo their hearts as well as their heads.

Most consultants present a dry, dreary, logical narrative that doesn't compel prospects to sign on the dotted line. An injection of life and emotion is needed. Your job is to weave a persuasive story that demonstrates your awareness of your prospects' emotions as well as their thoughts. The underpinnings of emotional persuasion were captured succinctly by Blair Warren, author of *The One Sentence Persuasion Course,* in 27 words:

> *"People will do anything for those who encourage their dreams, justify their failures, allay their fears, confirm their suspicions, and help them throw rocks at their enemies."*

Your persuasive story begins in the Situation section of your Context Document, where you confirm the client's suspicions by stating what the problem is. Yes, Yusimi told you the problem, but seeing it in black and white written out by someone else is affirming.

Then you include a single sentence that makes all the difference in the world. It sounds something like…

"Given the expansion of Sereus Dough's product line, it's almost unavoidable that your croissant throughput rates have declined."

That handful of words has simultaneously justified their failures (the declines were unavoidable) and thrown rocks at their enemies (those wacky marketing people over-expanded the product line).

Your persuasive story continues with the Desired Outcomes section. A typical consultant describes the objectives as deliverables that the client will receive in the future. Something like, "We will deliver a

comprehensive recommendations presentation at the conclusion of this initiative." You, however, are going to encourage your prospect's dreams by stating a future state (not a deliverable) *in present tense*. It looks like this:

"At the end of this project, Sereus Dough Inc. has a robust, reliable plan for achieving higher throughput rates and lower maintenance times."

It's amazing how much more emotionally powerful that Desired Outcomes statement is, rather than a dry promise of deliverables.

At first glance, the Perceived Risks and Concerns section of your Context Document may appear to intensify your prospect's fears; however, that's not the case. Nothing is worse than a nebulous, unnamed anxiety. Labeling and confirming Yusimi's concerns puts them in a box—a box you're going to handle neatly in the full proposal.

The Value section of your Context Document bolsters Yusimi's dreams by confirming that pursuing his vision will confer concrete benefits to the business and to himself. In this section you'll recap the financial gain and the assumptions you used to calculate them, and you'll highlight the positive, personal impact the engagement will produce. The personal part may read something like…

"In addition to the monetary benefits, boosting the throughput rates will showcase the competency and operations savvy of the plant's senior management."

Agree on the Context Document Before Developing Your Proposal

When your Context Document is complete, secure agreement to that document from the *decision maker*. For instance, if the decision maker at Sereus Dough, Inc. is Yuri Yusimi, but you conducted your Context Discussions with his subordinates you'll invariably find Yusimi has a different perspective on the outcomes or concerns. That's why it's vitally important you gain Yusimi's approval *before* you submit a formal proposal.

Clients are as consistent in their direction as a three-year-old chasing a cat. Add multiple stakeholders and you've got a party of disagreeing, cat-chasing toddlers. If the client is going to change his mind about what success means, or if there isn't alignment among the client's team, you need to find that out as early as possible—not after you've spent time developing a proposal, and definitely not after you've started the project!

I see far too many consultants jump from shallow discovery conversations directly into a proposal. Then they're surprised when they don't close the project. Or, the consultant accepts a lip service agreement to the context, which is meaningless. Agreement means Yusimi (the decision maker) says, "Yes, I want to increase throughput on the croissants line, and I believe your help is worth about $1.2 million and could set me up for a promotion. Maybe I'll be promoted to bagels!"

Don't be surprised if it takes a round or two of revisions to get your Context Document right and total buy-in from the powers-that-be at your prospect.

If you anticipate that inserting a stage before you submit your proposal slows the whole process down, you're absolutely right.

How many times have you had a prospect call you all flushed with excitement about a potential project and, after you spend hours (or days or weeks) developing a proposal, the prospect mysteriously goes AWOL? That happens because you're rushing the process; because the prospect isn't *confirming* from the outset that the project will definitely commence and that you're more than just a consideration. Clients rarely rush into the large, highly lucrative projects you want to win.

The two-stage method flushes out tire-kickers who are only looking for background information and are happy to eat up your time in the process. More importantly, investing upfront time in discovery gives prospects the sense that you're looking out for their best interests rather than yours.

The end result of slowing down the process is that when you do get to the point of submitting a proposal and negotiating the contract, trust is high, and the likelihood of winning the project is far, far greater than if you had rushed in with a proposal when your prospect first requested it.

Two Exceptions to the "Don't Rush" Rule

There are two cases when swift-like-a-hare trumps deliberate-like-a-tortoise:

1. *If a prospect calls you with absolutely burning urgency, has indicated with 100% certainty he will use you for the project, and he wants to get started immediately.* These types of situations don't come around too often for most consultants, but when they do, get the signature on the project and go.

   If you know for a fact that the project is kicking off immediately and that you're part of the team, then combine the

Context Document and Proposal into one step. You still need to conduct discovery, just shortcut the process.

2. *If you start the Context Discussion with the prospect and it quickly becomes clear he hates the process.* I find that about 5 percent of prospects are so averse to any sort of process that working through the Context Discussion before submitting a proposal is torture for them. If you run into one of those folks, feel free to abandon the process or abandon them. I usually choose to walk away because clients who hate structure and process tend to be unreasonably expensive to service.

Onward to Stage 2 of the Proposal Process

With agreement to your Context Document in hand, you're ready to craft the rest of your persuasive story in the form of a perfect, irresistible proposal.

CHAPTER 21

Creating a Perfect Proposal

Writing a proposal's easy when the prospect's head over heels at the thought of procuring your services. But most prospects aren't giddy at the thought of engaging you. That's why you need a killer proposal. One that generates *excitement* and *desire* and overcomes the prospect's natural reluctance to open his wallet.

TO AGREE TO YOUR PROJECT,
YOUR PROSPECT HAS TO FEEL SOME
PASSION ABOUT WORKING WITH YOU.

Toward the end of this chapter you'll see the outline of a simple, six-part structure that you can use for virtually any type and size of consulting project. Before we get there, consider this question:

what's the difference between a proposal that revs your prospect's engine versus one that gets ignored?

The answer's quite simple: Right-Side Up thinking.

Your proposal is not meant to highlight why you're great. It's designed to reassure prospects that you'll achieve their goal.

Most consultants think they're supposed to be the star of their proposal. Finally, they get to tell the story of why they are so awesome! "Look at our spiffy process. Look at our compelling case studies. Look at our impressive pedigrees."

The proposal *isn't* about you. It's about your prospect. That's why the three guidelines below heighten your likelihood to win virtually every project.

Three Guidelines for a Perfect Consulting Proposal

Note: The guidelines below will apply to all your proposals, with one exception: responding to a strict RFP (request for proposal) that specifies explicit section and format requirements.

1. Focus on Their Outcome, Not Your Tasks

The more your proposal dives into detail about your approach, the more you risk drifting into uninteresting "it's about me" territory and shifting everyone's focus to the activities rather than the results. Remember, your value comes from achieving an outcome, not from completing tasks.

What is undue detail? Anything beyond what is needed to assuage their fears. Prospects definitely want to see a robust process. A consultant who struts in with (flour) sacks full of bravado, and no support other than a few lines of *"I'll get this done"* usually gets tossed out on his ear.

PROVIDE ONLY ENOUGH DETAIL
TO CREATE CREDIBILITY AND
SUPPORT YOUR VALUE.

There's no exact formula for the amount of detail. Some buyers simply need to know, "First we'll analyze your data to find the throughput chokepoints…" Others need to know, "We're going to take the croissant baking data from the node simulator equipment and clean it for use by our analysts." Use your best judgment about this, but err on the side of *less* detail. If your prospects are feeling unsure, they'll ask you for more.

2. Provide Reassurance

Clients can be insecure. When you anticipate their objections, quiet their fears, and mitigate their perceived risks, you rise from a vendor to trusted ally. Thanks to the Context Discussion, you know most of the worries that are plaguing your prospect. That means your irresistible proposal can address your prospect's concerns explicitly in the approach and the contract structure.

For instance, if Yuri Yusimi at Sereus Dough, Inc. is afraid that his engineers will reject any suggestion from an outsider, you can include multiple work sessions with the engineers to enroll them. If he's worried your approach may not deliver results, you can give him a peek inside the black box and include case studies and testimonials.

If he expressed concern about who will actually be working on his project, include bios of the team. If he mentions ROI as a concern, show that your fees return a seven-to-one return on risk-adjusted value. Or create a fee structure that includes success fees, as explained in the next chapter.

EXPLICITLY ADDRESS CONCERNS WITH THE APPROACH AND FEES IN YOUR PROPOSAL

Those are just a few examples, of course. But no matter what the concern, you can respond to it by including language that shows you're attending to it. For instance, "...to address your concern about the validity of the data, I have built a test run into the process..."

Don't include everything plus the kitchen sink in your proposals. Again, just incorporate what's needed to ease Yusimi's worries and support his dreams. I don't include bios unless they're needed. The same goes for detailed processes, case studies, and other credentials that consultants often stuff into their proposals.

3. Offer Alternatives

When you submit one approach and one set of terms to Sereus Dough, you have a single shot at generating the necessary passion. You also receive very narrow feedback: whether or not they like that specific combination of approach and terms. Your prospect may give you a bit of direction on adjusting the approach or modifying the terms, but their guidance will be limited.

The perfect proposal finalizes the discovery process by presenting choices. Let that sink in for a moment. The perfect proposal isn't intended to synthesize your understanding into a single, ultimate submission. Instead, it affords you an opportunity to mold your offering into an even *more* obvious choice by soliciting your prospect's reaction to different combinations of *approaches* and *terms*.

When you offer three alternatives—i.e., distinct "bundles" of approaches and terms—to Sereus Dough, you'll receive *six times* the feedback—guidance on all three approaches and reactions to all three sets of terms.

Say you submit a proposal to Yusimi with three alternatives, priced at $155,000, $180,000 and $265,000. You could quickly find out one of the following about Yuri Yusimi:

- Those fees are way outside the realm of reality for him; or,

- He isn't fazed by fees north of $200,000 as long as you provide rapid-response access; or,

- He can't go higher than $180,000, but he's willing to give you the extra publicity you asked for and respond rapidly to your requests for information if you'll include the extra analysis described in the highest-price alternative.

That's the beauty of well-constructed alternatives. You discover more about your prospects' true desires and risk tolerance. You'll find out what methodologies best reduce their concerns and, based on that, what fears are most pronounced. Plus, you'll learn what terms, including pricing, are acceptable, and what are out of bounds.

Your prospects' reactions to the alternatives will suggest trades that benefit both of you. For instance, I sometimes trade a small fee reduction or a slightly expanded scope for quick turnaround from the client. Since receiving information and approvals from the client within 48 hours keeps my team efficient, improves outcomes and boosts margins, that's usually a smart trade.

After hearing Yusimi's comments on the alternatives, you assemble a final offering that incorporates the approach elements he wants most (and is willing to pay for), and the trades you discussed.

Some consultants claim a proposal should be a summary document submitted after everything, from outcomes to approach to fees, has already been agreed to during conversations with the prospect. I've found this approach occasionally succeeds for longtime clients with whom you've established tremendous trust and candor. Usually, though, the "proposal is a summary" idea runs contrary to prospects' purchasing processes and isn't realistic.

That said, don't write proposals as fishing expeditions. Your alternatives should reflect your deep understanding of the prospect's needs based on a thorough discovery process.

Structuring Your Perfect Proposal

Now that you know the three guidelines to follow, you can wrap them in a proposal structure that you'll use consistently for every project. The four-to-five page format outlined below works well for engagements from $10,000 to $1 million.

Section 1: Context

In this section you simply reprise the six elements of the Context Document: Situation, Desired Outcomes, Indicators of Success, Perceived Risks and Concerns, Value and Parameters. Remember, you've already received agreement to these, so when Yusimi reads through the first page or so of your proposal his head is already nodding (in agreement, not sleepiness).

Section 2: Approaches

This is where you bake in various combinations of methods, steps, and processes. For instance, one variation could promise a bare-bones, streamlined approach. Another could add a test run to confirm data validity. A third might include bi-monthly site visits to review the croissant throughput *in situ*. With product tasting, of course.

Generally, each alternative approach should augment the previous one. This is less confusing to the prospect than three completely independent methodologies.

The very first line of each alternative approach should highlight the enhanced value you're providing. Start with the result, not the process. It might sound like this:

> "Alternative 2 includes everything in Alternative 1 and adds value by reassuring your engineers that the croissant line's throughput data is valid."

Then you go on to detail the extra steps you're taking that deliver the incremental value.

There are times when building up the value doesn't make sense. In those cases create a "core approach," then offer independent options that the prospect can opt to include or exclude. For instance, addressing the croissant line may be your core approach and adding butter or oleo or coconut oil might all be options (because Yusimi could choose any or all three).

Section 3: Logistics

This section clearly and succinctly outlines the nuts and bolts of the contract, and includes:

- *Timing*. Any milestones and key dates you agree to meet. For most projects with most clients this can be a sentence or two, or a table with a handful of milestones. Sometimes a simple graphic depicting the major stages of the project and the timing of each is helpful.

  You do *not* need to outline every step in the process and how many days or weeks each one will take. In fact, those details make your project very fragile and susceptible to problems during delivery.

- *Responsibilities*. What are you and Sereus Dough agreeing to do to support the project effort? This includes your response times, communication approach, schedule for providing project updates, and so forth. Sereus Dough may be held to data turnaround times, to communicating any major changes and to paying you expeditiously.

WHY IS YOUR PROPOSAL TITLED "HOW TO HIRE ME IN 3 STEPS"?

IT SEEMS TO HELP

- *Dependencies*. Clearly outline any steps you are taking that you can only complete (or start) after your client has done something first. For instance, you might say, "Rollout of the solution will begin after Sereus Dough approves the data we deliver from the test run." Or a more general dependency such as, "Each stage in the approach will be started after Sereus Dough gives approval in writing to our work in the preceding stage." Calling out a handful of key dependencies in writing protects you and the project.

Section 4: Terms (Fees and Conditions)

This is the second place in your proposal where you vary your offering. (The first was Section 2: Approaches.) Your approach is not the only way to allay a prospect's fears or encourage his dreams. There are many, many ways to play with terms that add value for you and for your clients. I highly suggest you explore them in your contracts. A few terms you can vary include:

- Access to you
- Availability
- Rights to future projects
- Cancelability
- Project duration
- Fee structure

- Incentives
- Process intrusiveness
- Publicity
- Responsiveness
- Flexibility in timing
- Schedule of fee payments

Once you've cooked up a few alternatives—i.e., combinations of approaches and terms—outline your fees for each alternative you're presenting. As noted in the bullet-list above, you can offer more than one fee structure. Chapter 22 explores the topic of fees and fee structures in depth.

Section 5: Signatures

This very short section contains an obvious place for Yusimi to indicate which alternative and any optional elements of your proposal he is selecting, and to sign the document. Believe it or not, I've occasionally left out the place for my prospect to select an alternative. After I received the signed proposals I had to call them and ask what they signed up for. Yikes! Don't mimic my mistake—include the entire signatures section.

Section 6: Support Material

In some proposals you may include appendices that give greater detail to an anticipated deliverable, biographies of team members, or additional contract language required by the prospect. For instance, I've done work with Department of Defense contractors that required pages and pages of paragraphs stipulating that I would not share my work with countries on the terrorist watch list.

Only include materials that are required by the prospect. Cramming extra case studies, your mission statement, firm values, references and other bulk is more likely to get you dismissed than hired.

Example of a Perfect Proposal

You can whip up a typical, six-section, irresistible proposal in a few hours that will inspire your prospects, soothe every area of concern and render them speechless with excitement at the thought of working with you. An example of an actual, irresistible proposal, with key points highlighted is available online: **The Perfect Proposal Template**.

Since most of the intellectually challenging pieces were completed when you were writing the Context Document, pulling together a proposal is generally straightforward—except, perhaps, pricing. The one aspect of proposals that I'm asked for advice on most often is, without a doubt, fees. Let's take a look at fees and fee structures now.

BONUS MATERIAL

Bonus Materials available at davidafields.com/winningclients

The Perfect Proposal Template

---------------- CHAPTER 22 ----------------

Pricing and
Fee Structures

Some clever diamond marketer started promoting the idea that an engagement ring should cost roughly two months of the groom's salary. My extensive research suggests roughly half the love-struck population thinks two *days* would have been a better target. (The other half ardently supports two *years*.) Either way, both the giver and receiver of the diamond have a reference point for how much moola is invested in the sparkly declaration of affection.

Consultants have no such yardstick. In fact, I think pricing is the most perplexing part of winning a consulting project. Obviously, you don't want to price yourself out of the engagement, but there's no point in leaving money on the table either. Plus, clients often equate

213

higher fees with higher quality, so a high fee can boost your credibility and increase trust. The fee you quote is a tricky, tricky decision.

Two Quick Pricing Tips

Let me make this a little easier by giving you two quick tips before we dig deep into the pricing question:

Pricing tip # 1:
Find out what the budget is up front.

Okay, that one's obvious, but it bears a mention because knowing the budget makes determining your fees much easier. The budget doesn't necessarily create a ceiling. (For instance, in the Pine Tree Banking example I talked about in Chapter 15, the client agreed to pay 55 percent more than he had originally budgeted.) However, it puts you in the right ballpark.

Pricing tip #2:
Trust your gut.

If you have a strong feeling that Yuri Yusimi over at Sereus Dough, Inc. won't pay a penny more than $125,000, don't let someone talk you into submitting alternatives that start at $175,000. That said, don't let fear hold you back from earning higher fees. As I'll explain in a moment, higher fees for the same project are often better for the client as well as for you.

Two Decisions and the Six,
Basic Fee Structures

Ready to explore the inner workings of fee structures? Good. Let's consider the croissant project you're discussing with Yusimi. Two decisions will guide your fee structure and, ultimately, the size of the checks you receive. The decisions are:

Decision #1: The Basis of Your Fees

How you *determine* your fees, not how you *quote* them to your prospect. The two options are:

- *Cost basis*: You determine your fees based on the *cost* to do the project. For example, the Sereus Dough project takes a team of analysts and consultants six months, and you use your monthly rate for each team member to calculate the fee.

- *Value basis*: You determine your fees based primarily or entirely on the *value* of the project to your prospect. For instance, you and Yusimi estimate that the value of your work on the croissant project is $1.2 million over three years, and you use this valuation to anchor your fee.

Decision #2: The Timing of Your Fees

When you determine the *final*, total fees for the project. Your two choices are:

- *Before:* You determine a fixed, final fee for the project *before* the project commences. For example, you quote Yusimi $150,000 for the project, regardless of how long the project takes.

- *After*: You determine the final fees *after* the project has concluded. For example, after Sereus Dough has consumed your final, croissant report, you calculate the fees.

The First Four Fee Structures

You can depict those two decisions in a Fee Quadrant chart as shown in the Figure 22-1, and four of the basic fee structures are immediately apparent. The amounts in the examples below are just for illustration. In a few pages, there are guidelines for determining what the specific fees should be for your projects.

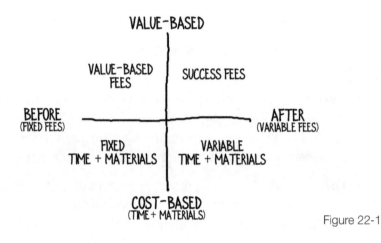

Figure 22-1

Fee Structure #1: Variable Time and Materials

Traditionally, most consulting projects have been paid for on the basis of actual costs; the lower right quadrant. For example, you charge $25,000 per month for your team. If the project is completed in six months, you charge $150,000. If the project requires an extra month, the total fees are $175,000.

Fee Structure #2: Fixed Time and Materials

At the lower left of the Fee Quadrant chart you are estimating your cost to complete the project, then quoting a fixed fee. For instance, you estimate the croissant project will occupy your team for six months. Your monthly cost is $20,000, but you charge your clients $25,000 per month. In this case you quote $150,000 and that's what you'll receive, no matter how long the engagement lasts.

Fee Structure #3: Fixed Value-Based Fees

The top left of the Fee Quadrant chart represents fixed fees that you've determined based on value. In this scenario, you tell Yusimi that the fee for the croissant project is $180,000, which you've determined using the $1.2 million estimated value as a guidepost. The fee you're quoting has little to do with the cost of the team or the duration of the project.

Fee Structure #4: Success Fees

In the top right quadrant you're paid based on the actual value you produce. This is sometimes called *Skin-in-the-Game*. For example, you agree your compensation will be five percent of the value of the incremental croissant throughput your project produces. If your project results in virtually no incremental croissants, you're going to lose some dough yourself. However, if you do a great job and the value of those additional pastries is $7 million, then your five percent earns you a tidy $350,000.

The Two, Hybrid Fee Structures

Fee Structure #5: Variable Time and Materials with a Cap

If Sally Scarlet, the purchasing director at Sereus Dough thinks she's clever, she might ask for a hybrid structure that pays $25,000 per month but caps consulting fees at $150,000. Many purchasers of consulting gravitate toward this structure because intuitively it seems to be the best of all worlds. Their intuition is leading them astray.

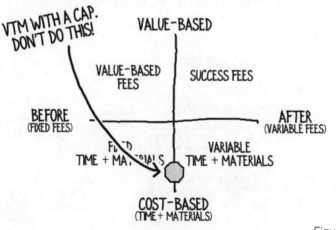

Figure 22-2

Variable Time and Materials with a Cap is the *worst* fee structure—for both the consultant *and* the client. I'm sure you quickly realize this structure could result in lower fees to you if the duration of the initiative is short, but if the engagement runs long your upside is limited by the cap. Doesn't sound very enticing, does it? This unattractive structure for consultants turns out to be a poor option for clients too. (For a detailed explanation as to why this structure is bad for clients, see pp. 179-181 in *The Executive's Guide to Consultants*.)

Fee Structure #6: Fixed Value-Based Fees with a Bonus

Finally, you could offer a fixed, value-based fee with success fees worked in as a bonus based on the actual results. For instance, if you and Yusimi agreed the goal is a 20 percent increase in throughput, you could reduce your fixed fee (based on value) from $180,000 to $150,000 and earn a $60,000 bonus if you hit or exceed the throughput goal. Sereus Dough only pays the bonus if your project is successful (in which case, the extra $60,000 is a pittance compared to their gain) and you're earning a higher margin for your proven value.

The six different fee possibilities on the croissant project are captured in Figure 22-3.

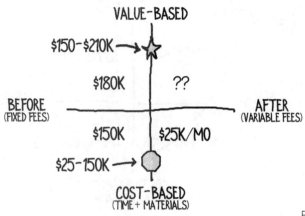

POSSIBLE FEES ON THE CROISSANT PROJECT

Figure 22-3

Which Fee Structure is Best?

All else being equal, assuming you're good at what you do, your margin will increase as you move clockwise around the quadrant chart from lower right to upper right. I call this the Premium Curve. The exact same project (again, assuming you're successful) will yield far more margin for you with a hybrid, value-based fee structure than with a variable, cost-based structure.

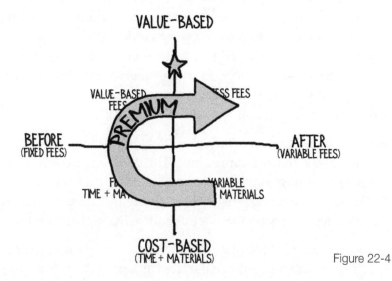

Figure 22-4

How do you earn the right to propose value-based fee structures? By building up trust; i.e., by being perceived as far more likely to put the client first, deliver outstanding results, and minimize the risk of harm. Conversely, when you offer the same skills and value as other consultants and simply execute the client's directions, you look like an outsourced commodity. That's not a route to high margins.

In most cases, a hybrid, value-based fee structure will be the best bet for your project. If Yusimi is savvy, he'll realize that structure reduces his risk, confirms your confidence in your approach, and increases the likely payout from his investment.

Why do I generally recommend a hybrid fee structure rather than pure, success fees? Because most clients won't enter into a contract based 100% on success fees, and that's just as well. Unless you structure them correctly, success-fee contracts are fraught with undue risk on both sides. If you are seriously considering using this type of contract, I recommend you review pages 182-185 of *The Executive's Guide to Consultants*.

An Exception: Fees for Ongoing Advice

Please note: all six of the structures outlined above are for *project work*—in other words, a well-defined task with a well-defined endpoint. They are not the fee structures you would use for ongoing, advisory services. Ongoing advisory work is typically paid for as a stipend. (Some people call this a retainer.) In other words, Yusimi will pay $10,000 per month for you to give ongoing input on the Ohio plant's operations. Perhaps you agree to six-month blocks, which you can renew at the end of each block.

If you're doing advisory work, don't let your stipend agreement turn into a fees-for-hours arrangement. The company's contract janitors get paid an hourly wage—time-and-a-half for nights and weekends. CEOs get paid a salary—big dollars for big thinking, no matter how many or few hours it takes. Act like the CEO, not the janitor.

If you are engaged for ongoing advisory work, you may unearth a specific need that should be handled as a project. In this case, draw up a separate proposal for the project and quote those fees separately from your periodic stipend. I have seen far too many cases where commingling advisory work and project work has led to unhappy clients and consultants.

How Much Should You Charge?

Now you're at the nub of the matter. What fee, exactly, should you charge for your project? This is one of the most common questions I'm asked by consultants.

If you're going to use a cost-based fee structure, then the answer is easy. Set a rate based on your level of expertise compared to other players in the market. Either estimate the time it will take to complete the project and set a fixed fee, or do the project and earn your

fee based on the time it actually takes. You may also want to consider Yusimi's perception of what it would cost him to use other resources, such as internal staff.

In addition, if you're sticking with cost-based structures, you'll want to pay particular attention to utilization rates, overhead, desired profitability, and similar metrics. Since I don't advocate using a cost-based fee structure, I haven't included detailed discussions of these points.

If you're opting to present value-based fees, then the answer is a bit trickier. Obviously, the first consideration is the value of the project, which you established during the Context Discussion.

A reasonable rule of thumb to get your thinking started is a seven-to-one return on risk-adjusted value.

In other words, if the value of *your* work to help Sereus Dough Inc. improve its croissant throughput is estimated at $1.2 million over three years, then a reasonable stick in the sand is around $170,000 or so. The seven-to-one rule of thumb is a *starting point*, not an exact, scientific formula. I might consider $180,000 (as I did in the example of Fee Structure #3) or even $200,000, both of which still give an outstanding return.

What's your reaction to the $200,000 bogey? Do you anticipate Yusimi would suffer traumatic shock if he saw that fee and kick you out of his office? If so, think deeply about whether that's *really* what Yuri Yusimi's reaction would be or whether your fear and insecurity are talking—often, it's your insecurity. In which case, take a deep breath and stick to $200,000.

However—and this is important—if your work during the Context Discussion tells you Yusimi will never pay more than $175,000, or your gut instinct tells you that's his limit, price the project at $175,000, close the project and walk away a happy consultant.

Let's consider a scenario in which you estimate the project will demand a full year of effort from your entire team. In this case, $200,000 might not even cover your costs, and your choices are to either offer Yusimi a lower return or pass on the project.

Keep in mind that you're going to be presenting *multiple* prices, as discussed in Chapter 21. If $180,000 is your stick in the sand, then you may want to offer three combinations of approaches and terms with fees as follows:

- $155,000 (your "low fee" option)
- $180,000
- $265,000 (all the bells and whistles)

(For more ideas on how to arrange the pricing of three alternatives, download **Five Pricing Strategies that Will Win You More Projects at Higher Fees**.)

What About the Competition?

If every other consultant is charging $15,000 to $20,000 per month and willing to cap their fees at $120,000, is it realistic to walk in with a $180,000 fee based on value? In two words: it depends.

Yes: You can command far higher fees, *provided* you've built up enough trust and you are perceived as a higher value solution. ("Higher value" generally means you are trusted to deliver a better result.)

No: You'll lose the project if you don't have a strong relationship or reputation or credibility that outshines competitors.

By and large, if you're setting fees based on value, your best bet is to ignore the competition and focus on the client. Yuri Yusimi, not your competitors, determines whether you win a project and how much you'll make. Sure, if competitors are coming in at $10,000 and you're asking for $100,000, you're not likely to be awarded the engagement. However, I've routinely won projects with fees that are 30 percent to three times higher than competitors, and you can, too.

If you set your fees based on market averages, you'll achieve average revenue—at best. However, if your fees are commensurate with the superior value you're offering your client, then you're more apt to win high margin projects.

Are High Fees Ethical?

Finally, let's address a point that may be nagging at you—or you think is so loathsome to Yusimi that he could wrap you in layers of butter and drop you in a commercial mixer. Is it ethical and fair to ask for higher fees based on value than you would charge based on your costs?

Yes.

All things equal, a higher fee for the same project is not only better for you, it's better for Sereus Dough. Here's why:

HIGHER FEES GIVE YOU THE ROOM TO DO WHATEVER IT TAKES TO MAKE THE PROJECT A SUCCESS.

If you're operating on a razor thin margin, you're unlikely to spend any extra time or effort on a project. You'll resist changes to the project plan even when they're warranted, and you'll have to negotiate a change order (ugh!) every time any additional work is needed. In contrast, with a healthy margin, you have the freedom to rework, adjust, and give "extra" to achieve the desired outcome, while still turning a profit.

Yusimi's goal is to achieve an *outcome*, not to spend a certain amount of money. When you're focused on outcomes, you realize your fees could often double or even triple and still be outweighed by a small increase in the client's success.

Let's recap: you've figured out your fee structure, written your fees into the proposal, and submitted it to Yuri Yusimi. No doubt he'll call you in a matter of hours to exclaim breathlessly, "I emailed a copy of the signed proposal last night and wired money to your account. You're my favorite consultant. Let's get started!"

Or... maybe not. Chances are he's going to put your negotiation skills to the test. Fortunately, you're about to learn five best practices for negotiating consulting contracts.

BONUS MATERIAL

Bonus Materials available at davidafields.com/winningclients

Five Pricing Strategies that Will Win
You More Projects at Higher Fees

CHAPTER 23

Five Ways to Negotiate Like a Pro

If you love haggling with car salesmen, then nego-
tiation may be your favorite part of developing
new business. On the other hand, if you get
the jitters telling the supermarket cashier
that the potatoes rang up at $29.99 instead
of $2.99, then you may do anything to
avoid negotiating.

TAKE THIS PROPOSAL, IT'S A BEAUT!

Either way, it's part of the process. It's
extremely rare that you submit a proposal
and the decision maker signs it without ask-
ing for some change or concession. Fortunately, it's not hard to be
good at consulting negotiations. Remember, you and your prospect
aren't labor lawyers slugging it out over five-year union contracts.
By and large, this is a friendly discussion, and you start out 90 percent aligned.

Let's say you've sent your proposal to Yuri Yusimi at Sereus Dough,
Inc. and now you're meeting with him to close the deal. Your meeting may start off like this:

⁓⁓⁓

YURI YUSIMI: "Hey, thanks for coming in. I didn't really have a chance to look through this document you sent in advance, but I printed it out." (He quickly flips to the page with fees,) "Oooh, this is way too much! Hmm…" (scanning through some other pages) "I don't think we're going to need this second assessment. And you're going to need to take all of this through purchasing, of course."

⁓⁓⁓

Hey, what happened to value? To trust? Gosh, to common courtesy? And now the purchasing department has a say?

Fortunately, you can conquer even the most difficult negotiation by remembering the Three Cs of negotiation: stay Calm, be Confident in yourself and your offering, and always Consider your prospect's point of view. In practical terms, the Three Cs translate into five best practices:

1. Always Deal with the Decision Maker

Some people say *only* deal with the decision maker, but that's naïve. If Yusimi's lieutenants have been tasked with negotiating the deal, then you can't simply ignore them. You work with them while maintaining your peer-to-peer link with Yusimi. In conversation it sounds like this:

⁓⁓⁓

YURI YUSIMI: "I only have about five minutes, but I've asked the line manager and engineering manager to come in, and I'd like you to work this through with them. They'll be able to decide whether your group can help."

YOU: "Okay. Since we only have a couple of minutes, do you mind if I ask a quick process question?"

YURI YUSIMI: "Sure. What is it?"

YOU: "Who ultimately will make the decision on whether to bring us in? Does the engineering manager or line manager have the authority to sign, or will that be you?"

YURI YUSIMI: "Well, ultimately it will be me. I'm the one that has to approve projects like this. But I want you to work out the details with those guys first."

YOU: "Absolutely. I'm happy to work with your team. But before I finalize the details, I'll want to discuss them with you, since you're ultimately responsible."

YURI YUSIMI: "Sure. That's no problem. Start working through the process with my managers, and I'll look forward to talking with you again in a couple of days."

A Potential Hiccup: The Procurement Department

I'm often asked how to deal with procurement departments when, for whatever reason, you end up in their sights. The answer is simple: help Yuri Yusimi retain his authority. In other words, work with procurement, but keep Yusimi involved. Much of your conversation will sound exactly like the one we just went through. Below is an example:

---*mm*---

YURI YUSIMI: "At this point, you'll need to work through the procurement department. They take a look at all consulting agreements. I know it's a pain, but that's how it works."

YOU: "Okay. No problem, I have to work with procurement groups all the time. Just so I'm clear, though, who ultimately signs for the project. Is it you or someone in corporate?"

YURI YUSIMI: "Oh, I sign for it. It's coming from my budget."

YOU: "Great. I'll submit the proposal to you and copy procurement. Then I'll supply procurement as much information as I can. Sometimes they ask for things I don't have, because you can't buy consulting the way you buy widgets."

YURI YUSIMI: "I totally get it, but they don't always see it that way."

YOU: "Well, let's wait to worry about procurement problems until they come up. I'll cooperate with them as much as possible and if we run into roadblocks, I'll let you know so you can lean on them a bit."

YURI YUSIMI: "Yeah, I do have to lean on them sometimes."

YOU: "Sounds great."

---*mm*---

Ironically, when you've been pushed off to someone else, your prospect becomes your best ally. After all, he *wants* the project. Therefore, when you're at an impasse with the procurement group or a subordinate, you ask Yusimi for help breaking the logjam. For example:

~~~

YOU: "Hi, Yuri. Do you have a minute? I could use some advice. What's the best way to work through your procurement process with the least amount of pain and delays?"

Or...

YOU: "Hi, Yuri. Our proposal is stuck somewhere in your procurement process and we're sort of stymied. At this point I think you'll need to give your purchasing folks a call. You and I are in agreement on how we want to do this but, well, you know how it goes. They're just tied to their standard rules."

~~~

2. The Strategic Delay

Before addressing *any* of your prospect's concerns, give him a chance to lay out all of the obstacles between you and a signed contract. I call this the Strategic Delay. It's very easy in theory, but surprisingly difficult in practice because we have such a strong urge to immediately respond to whatever the prospect brings up. Fighting that urge will serve you extremely well. Your allies in the struggle are two words: "*What else?*"

~~~

YURI YUSIMI: "You know, I'm a bit worried that my people aren't going to be able to do this. They're good, but they're not the strongest team I've worked with."

YOU: "Okay. I hear you. You've got some concerns about your internal capabilities. What else? What other issues popped up when you reviewed my proposal?"

~~~

Exercising patience like this surfaces the full list of objections and ensures there's nothing hidden that could trip you up. For some reason, prospects often initiate negotiations with semi-important issues and hold back their make-or-break issues. Consciously or unconsciously, they want to see how you deal with a few rocks thrown your way before they fire their heavy cannons.

If you allow yourself to fall into drawn-out negotiation over the first couple of topics Yusimi raises, he may simply grow weary of the process and turn down the proposal before you get to the larger, underlying objection.

In addition, the Strategic Delay safeguards you against becoming defensive. Inserting a bit of space between Yusimi's objection and your response creates a natural buffer, and you're less likely to blurt out a knee-jerk, defensive response.

Waiting for the complete list of concerns before diving in also allows you to be choiceful about which issues you'll tackle and in what order. Concede the easy points at the beginning, then work your way to more contentious issues. That way you're creating positive momentum, acting as a collaborator, earning some bargaining chips, and letting Yusimi expend his negotiating energy on issues that cost you little or nothing. When you start with the least onerous objections you'll often find the more challenging ones evaporate almost magically.

3. Seek to Understand

Once you get all of Yusimi's concerns, objections and requests for changes out in the open, you can tackle them one by one. Starting with the *easiest* issue, you'll first ask for clarification to ensure you understand the thinking behind his concern. Do this *every time*, even with concerns that are simple to address. It's much easier to remember and stick to your process if you don't pick and choose when to apply it.

Your exchange sounds something like this:

YOU: "Okay, so you have some concerns about the fees and you think the timing of phase two could delay your product launch. You're also concerned about how your engineers will react to the interviews, and you've said that we need all findings delivered in French and Swahili. And finally, you raised the non-cancellation clause as a concern.

"Is there anything else that could get in the way of us moving forward, or if we address those concerns, are we good to go?"

YURI YUSIMI: "No, that's it. If we can do that, we're good."

YOU: "Okay, great. Let's start with the language concerns. I assume you want findings in Swahili so that Hodari's group can read through them. Is that right?"

YURI YUSIMI: "Yes. And, well, actually, we're in the midst of a multi-cultural initiative and we're ensuring everything we produce is in three languages."

YOU: "Okay. Got it! Is there anything else we need to do to help you meet your multi-cultural goals?"

YURI YUSIMI: "No, just produce the findings in French and Swahili."

Now, I would hope that you found out about the multi-cultural program during the Context Discussion or some other conversation, but surprises do crop up. And that's why you always seek to understand. In addition, each deeper reason behind an objection is an opportunity to improve the project and strengthen your bond with your prospect.

4. Defend Your Prospect

Every book and course on negotiation teaches you not to become defensive. They're right, of course. No matter what Yusimi brings up, taking it personally and assuming a defensive stance isn't going to hold sway. Since it's easier to avoid becoming defensive if you have something else to put in its place, let's bring Right-Side Up thinking into play yet again: *always start by defending your prospect during negotiations.*

In other words, rather than launching into a passionate, well-researched defense of why your proposal is best for Yusimi, you'll have much better luck if you start by defending his point of view. You sought first to understand; now, acknowledge the reasons his position could be correct.

Suppose, for instance, he's challenging your no-cancellation clause. Start your discussion of the clause by arguing *Yusimi's* position. When your initial response embraces his claims, he feels validated and is far more likely to accept your final reasoning. And yes, you do follow with your rationale for the no-cancellation clause.

Once you've overtly pleaded Yusimi's side of the disagreement, you'll find him surprisingly willing to adopt your alternative, even if the rationale for your position isn't overwhelming. Here's an example:

mm

YURI YUSIMI: "This no-cancellation clause is never going to work. We could never enter into a contract that isn't cancellable."

YOU: "I understand your reticence on that clause. It probably feels as though that shifts all the risk onto you. After all, what if we totally screw up along the way?"

YURI YUSIMI: "That's right."

YOU: "Well, that's why we guarantee our work. If *anything* goes wrong, we'll take care of it, no matter what it takes or what it costs. But let's say you decide to shift strategy along the way and the project's no longer relevant. That's actually a risk to us, right?"

YURI YUSIMI: "Yeah. I don't think that will happen, but I see what you're saying."

YOU: "So, actually all the risk was on us and this just balances it out. If your strategy does shift, we can redirect the resources at any time."

YURI YUSIMI: "Oh. Okay. That's unusual, but I get it."

mm

5. Make Smart Trades

Imagine walking into negotiations hoping your project will earn you a 30 percent margin and leaving the table with a deal that nets you 40 percent instead. Sound crazy? It's neither crazy nor even far-fetched when you master the art of making trades.

DO YOU HAVE ANY MORE BUDGET?

GO FISH

Your starting point on making trades happened during the Context Discussion. When you uncovered Yusimi's perceived risks and concerns, you also revealed opportunities to creatively reallocate risk. Your first set of trades was contained in your proposal. You developed approach alternatives that created added value for your client *and* mitigated and/or reallocated some of the risks. During negotiation you'll be able to bring more trades to the table to close the deal.

For instance, let's say Yusimi is worried that the project could take too long and delay his product launch. You could offer an alternative that compresses the timeline by two weeks and adds resource triggers. If a milestone is missed, you'll add around-the-clock resources to bring the project back onto the fast track. In return (i.e., the trade), you are awarded a higher fee or access to another project or some other benefit.

Smart trades shift negotiation from compromises to win-win.

Too many people think negotiation is all about making concessions. It's not. Walk into every proposal discussion with a handful of trades in mind that could add value for the client *and* you.

The Fee Objection—A Special Case?

How often have you run into a response to your proposal like this one:

—*mm*—

YURI YUSIMI: "This looks good. I really want to do this project and get started with it, but your fees are just too high."

—*mm*—

Uh oh, the dreaded fee objection. Objections over fees actually *aren't* a special case. You can handle them using the same five best practices outlined above: ensure Yusimi is the decision maker, not a subordinate; utilize the Strategic Delay to avoid being drawn into a fees discussion too early; solicit additional information to determine what's driving the fee concern; defend Yusimi's point of view; and, if necessary, make smart trades.

Congratulations! You've attracted a prospect, built a relationship with him, turned the conversation to a specific issue, conducted discovery then proposed and successfully negotiated the project. You're ready to cash the check, right? Oh, wait a second... where's the check?

CHAPTER 24

Living the Dream

Is that everything? Yes. Well, almost. You attracted prospects thanks to your high-impact message and your powerful, visibility building. You transitioned relationships into opportunities and, after a deep discovery process, you gained agreement to your Context Discussion. You even submitted a proposal and negotiated the approach, terms, and fees with your client. What's left? Why don't you have a signed contract yet?

You have to ask for the business!

It's your responsibility to make sure Yuri Yusimi knows his next action: *sign the proposal and send it back.* Some consultants are uncomfortable with this step. Don't be. You put in the work; you built trust; you established value. What are you waiting for?

If you're hoping the client will close the deal for you, you may wait in vain. Many a project has foundered on this final obstacle to success. The two examples below will give you the language you need to close the deal.

—◁◁◁◁—

Example 1:

> YURI YUSIMI: "This looks good."
>
> YOU: "Great. Just sign the proposal and we'll start things rolling on Monday."

Example 2:

> YURI YUSIMI: "This looks good."
>
> YOU: "Excellent. Do you have any remaining questions, issues or concerns about the proposal?"
>
> YURI YUSIMI: "No, I think you've done a good job taking care of all of my issues."
>
> YOU: "Thank you. The next step is for us to have a fully executed agreement. What's the best way to get a copy of the proposal with your signature on it?"

—◁◁◁◁—

It's as simple as that. But if your client wants to revise the proposal, there's no need to panic; quickly make the revisions and have another negotiation discussion. And then, if everything looks good, what do you do? *You ask for the business.* You MUST ask the client to move forward in working with you.

Oh, and there's one last thing.

Make Dust Fly

Early in my consulting career I learned what my mentors called, "making dust fly." As soon as you win a project you need to show some very obvious activity to make it clear the project is in motion and valuable activities are underway. Why? Because between the time a client gives approval for a project and the time the project actually gets underway is dangerous territory.

Even after they've signed your proposal, clients are fretting about their decision. *"Should I have signed this? Was this the right choice? Is this going to work out?"* There's always the chance that buyer's remorse sets in and they cancel the project before you get it up and running. By immediately involving Yusimi in project activity you shift his internal dialogue from *"Should I do this project?"* to *"The project's in motion. What's next?"* That's a critical shift.

Clouds of flying dust look like commitment and momentum, which are closely linked. And when you show that the project has commitment and momentum, then Yusimi's buy-in is solidified, and any chance of his backing out evaporates.

Shouldn't You Get Paid Before You Jump In?

You may be wondering how you make dust fly without doing considerable work before the first check arrives. Fair question, with two answers.

First, if Yusimi has agreed to an upfront payment (and I certainly hope he did!) and you believe Sereus Dough, Inc. is a reputable company, then act on good faith. Start working with the understanding that your first check is going to arrive soon.

Second, remember that clouds of dust are best created by highly visible activities and prodding the *client* into action too. Working your tail off at the start of a project, without Yusimi seeing your efforts, does you no favors. Instead, take very noticeable steps such as sending a project launch letter, setting up a project portal or sending out contact information for the team.

Fortunately, virtually every project requires information from the client. Within an hour of receiving approval, send out a detailed information request. Yusimi may forward the request to his subordinates, and suddenly a host of minions are busy collecting data for you. Dust is flying, the project is in motion, Yusimi is committed, and you're embarked on another successful engagement.

Living the Dream

Congratulations! You're cashing checks, working hard and enjoying the extraordinary life independent consulting has to offer.

Just beware of taking your eyes off the ball now that you're in "delivery" mode. If you don't consistently work *at* your relationships while you're working *for* your clients, your big success may last about four months.

I have faith in you. I know you're going to keep your business development engine turned on and humming along at all times. You'll be attracting and building strong relationships every week, month and year. You know the Six Steps aren't a one-time shot of steroids, but rather a daily exercise routine that, over time and consistently practiced, will make your business healthy, wealthy, strong, and happy.

May I offer one final piece of advice? Be patient. Go at the process one step at a time, and always begin with (and return to) thinking Right-Side Up. If you learn to align yourself with your prospects' perspective, you'll not only lose your anxiety about developing new business; you'll put yourself miles ahead of your competition in your prospects' eyes.

That's because there's a very fine line between the successful professional and the struggling one. To cross that line you don't need more expertise or more experience, but rather something far more valuable: the ability to plant yourself firmly and squarely in the other person's shoes *and stay there for as long as it takes.*

No client has ever objected when a consultant understands him better and cares about him more. So if you want to start living the dream, take action and take care. And start doing it *now.*

David A. Fields

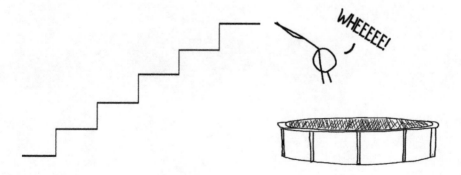

Index

About the Author

Best-selling author and acclaimed speaker, consultant, and mentor David A. Fields works with individual consultants and consulting firms across the globe that are eager to accelerate growth, increase profit and create lucrative, lifestyle-friendly practices. He has guided consultancies ranging from one-person startups to the consulting divisions of some of the world's largest companies.

David still advises corporate clients too. After climbing the ranks to become a partner at a prestigious consulting firm in Connecticut, David co-founded Ascendant Consulting, where he has attracted clients such as Abbott Laboratories, Church & Dwight, FMC, Warner Home Video, and many others.

He also leads the Ascendant Consortium, a unique, "general contractor" model in which David acts as both a client and consultant on the same project.

David received his Bachelor's and Master's degrees from Carnegie Mellon (go plaid!). He is a hockey fanatic and eats egregious amounts of chocolate... but you probably knew that already.

Contact David at david@davidafields.com to inquire about having him work with your firm or speak at your event.

Free resources are available for you at davidafields.com/winning-clients.

CPSIA information can be obtained
at www.ICGtesting.com
Printed in the USA
BVHW031452230719
554166BV00001B/1/P

9 781683 501640